MASSACRE AT MALMÉDY

"Whiting's description of battles is superb."
—*The New York Times*

"Lively reading."—*Library Journal*

"A penetrating character study."—*Navy Times*

"Does much to recall the history of a grim period, the tensions and momentary hopes of troops, the in-fighting among allied commanders, especially after Montgomery was given command."

—*Best Sellers*

By the same author

Fiction
THE FRAT WAGON
JOURNEY TO NO END
THE MIGHTY FALLEN
LEST I FALL

Military History
DECISION AT ST VITH
PATTON—A CRITICAL BIOGRAPHY
48 HOURS TO HAMMELBURG

Linguistics
SPIEGELGESPRÄCHE—A TEXTBOOK
FOR INTERPRETERS

Massacre
at
Malmédy

THE STORY OF JOCHEN PEIPER'S BATTLE GROUP
ARDENNES, DECEMBER, 1944

by
CHARLES WHITING

day books

A Division of STEIN AND DAY/Publishers/New York

FIRST DAY BOOKS EDITION 1981

First published in hardcover by
Stein and Day/*Publishers*

Copyright © 1971 by Charles Whiting
Library of Congress Catalog Card No. 71-150521
ISBN: 0-8128-7023-9
All rights reserved
Printed in the United States of America

Stein and Day/*Publishers*/ Scarborough House
Briarcliff Manor, New York 10510

CONTENTS

ILLUSTRATIONS

MAPS

GLOSSARY

Ami	Derogatory term used by Germans for an American: abbreviation of Ámerikaner
Kampfgruppe	Battle group
Leibstandarte	Hitler's personal SS Regiment
Obersturmbannfuehrer	Lieutenant-Colonel of SS
Pioniere	German military engineers
Reichsfuehrer	National Leader—title given to leading Nazi civilians
Reichskanzeler	Chancellery
Reichswehr	Title of German Army between 1919 and 1933
SS Reitersturm	SS Cavalry Regiment
Waffen SS	Armed SS—as opposed to the Totenkopfverbande, the guards for concentration camps, etc.
Wehrmacht	Title of Germany Army after Hitler's takeover

INTRODUCTION

At dawn on 17 December, 1944, the first camouflaged tanks of the German point began to nose their way into the little Belgian border village of Büllingen. Everything was still. Not a sign of the enemy anywhere. Not even sentries! Satisfied that the Ardennes village contained neither American anti-tank guns or tanks, the German tank commanders rapped out swift orders to their drivers and gunners. In the roar of the tank diesels, they cried *'Los!'*

Swiftly the Panthers gathered speed. The gunners swung round their machine-guns. They were rolling down the cobbled street now. On both sides the lights started to go on in the little white-painted houses. Blackout regulations were thrown to the wind. There were shouts of alarm, rage—fear. The first German tank opened up. Machine-gun slugs splattered against the walls of the first house. Plaster and stone flew in all directions. An *Ami* ran out half dressed and was shot down before he could raise his carbine. A second followed him, slewing to halt and hitting the stone cobbles hard. The third raised his hands.

Within minutes it was all over. Two hundred Americans surrendered. The rest fled westwards in broken confusion, impotent against this iron monster which had appeared so frighteningly and suddenly in their midst. Büllingen was German. After twenty-four hours of futile attempts at breakthrough, *Obersturmbannfuhrer* Jochen Peiper, commander of the premier regiment of the premier division of the German Army, *Die Leibstandarte*,[1] had penetrated the US lines in the Belgian Ardennes. The real Battle of the Bulge had begun.

On that grey, damp misty morning Colonel Peiper, at 29 one of the youngest regimental commanders in the German Army, began one of the most daring and at the same time one of the most far-reaching operations of the war. It took him and his picked formation of 5,000 élite soldiers deep into the Allied camp, threatening not only

---

[1] Usually translated as *'Adolph Hitler's bodyguard'—the 1 SS Panzer Division.*

vital communication centres and supply dumps but also the person of the US 1st Army commander himself, General Courtney Hodges, who had to flee his headquarters, from which he controlled nearly half a million soldiers, in face of the threat posed by Peiper's swift moving panzers. In the end Peiper was surrounded and beaten by the concentrated force of two and half elite American divisions.

But Peiper's story did not end with his last-ditch stand in the encircled village of La Gleize. It carried on for years after the war and was only ended when the babies who were born in the last year of the conflict were joining the Army themselves. For Peiper and his soldiers were accused of one of the major massacres of World War Two—the infamous 'Malmédy Massacre' which over the years was going to occupy the attentions of thousands of people who had never even heard of Malmédy prior to December, 1944. In fact, Peiper and his handful of survivors from the last-ditch stand in the hill village of La Gleize were to become an international issue, with which archbishops, editors, historians, senators and presidents would have to concern themselves and which, in the final analysis, discredited American military justice.

This, then, is the story of those bloody seven days in the third week in December, 1944, when Peiper and his Five Thousand were the men who could bring about a change in the whole course of the war in the West. It is also the story of the long weary years of trial and torture that followed those heady victorious days of December, 1944. It attempts to present no moral—save that we are all in one way or another—*guilty*.

Naturally a book of this kind cannot be written without help. A lot of people have helped me with it. But in particular, I should like to thank the following: Dr Maurice Delaval, that dentist-historian, to whom everyone who writes about the Battle of the Bulge must turn to in his dark Vielsalm surgery sooner or later. To Ambassador Eisenhower, son of the late President, who found time from his office to answer questions on a subject which is close to his heart; to Tom Stubbs, 36th Fighter Wing Librarian, always to be relied upon for information; to Major-General Sir Kenneth Strong, Eisenhower's former intelligence officer, a great source of help; Dr Günther Deschner of the German publishing house of Berthelsmann Ltd, a walking human computer on the last year of the war; Madame Lejeune of Büllingen who suffered so much herself in the Battle of the Bulge but who used her remarkable energy to organise witnesses for me—and naturally ex-*Obersturmbannfuehrer* Jochen Peiper himself, who for better or for worse has become part of the legend and the history of the Battle of the Bulge . . .

'Had he and I but met
By some old ancient inn,
We should have sat us down to wet
Right many a nipperkin!

But ranged as infantry,
And staring face to face,
I shot at him as he at me,
And killed him in his place.'

Thomas Hardy

Massacre
at
Malmédy

BOOK ONE
The Assault

Day One:
SATURDAY, 16 DECEMBER, 1944

'Auf wiedersehen, Herr Leutnant, see you in America!'

Anonymous soldier of 1SS
to an officer of Peiper's Group,
0530 hrs.

Soon it would be dawn. Here and there the night sky was lit up by a flash of pink and yellow on the horizon to the north. But the guns of the new offensive were too far away to be heard. Here the front lay quiet under a brooding winter silence.

On the horizon the occasional red flare bathed everything in its icy light. In their foxholes the sentries stared upwards. They stamped their frozen feet, remembering the warnings about contacting trench foot which had been drummed into them in the last few days. Their officers had said it was a punishable offence to contract it, now that some of the men in the combat outfits were deliberately cultivating it in order to get out of the line. Not that the lone sentries expected any combat here in the twisting front line which worked its way in and out of Belgium and Germany as it ran through the rugged Ardennes–West Eifel hills. They knew they were here to train and prepare for the day when they would be sent from this 'Ghost Front' to one of the 'hot' ones to north or south.

Behind the front line, the rear echelon slept. There were only nine more days to Christmas, absolutely the last one of the war, everybody was saying. The 'Kraut' was finished, kaput. Why worry about the war? In the huts erected in the middle of the frozen fir forests, and in the dirty-white houses with their manure heaps in front of the kitchen windows and a crucifix in every room, the young soldiers of the unblooded divisions guarding the 'ghost front' tossed and turned in their sleep.

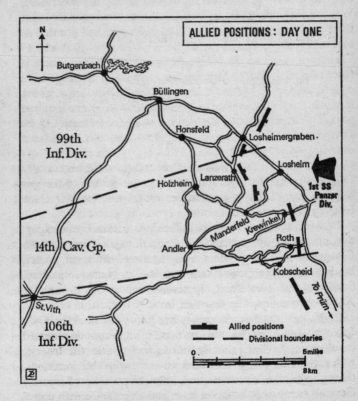

But here and there behind the line some soldiers were awake, and worried. Back at the command post of the 99th Infantry Division in the little Belgian frontier village of Butgenbach that Saturday morning, staff officers were awake and busy, their flagging energy renewed by endless cigarettes and cups of strong black coffee. The young captains and majors of this green division, which had only been in the Ardennes since November, knew that the dawn might bring trouble. Further to the north, the veteran 2nd Infantry Division was passing through the 99th's lines on its way to attack the Roer area. When that attack got underway, Intelligence had predicted that there might be 'a spoiling raid' (as Intelligence had phrased it) somewhere along the Division's twenty mile front. But where? Their positions ran the length of the Siegfried Line where it faced Belgium, down to the tiny village of Lanzerath, a collection of white-painted stone houses and a few farms, whose inhabitants spoke German and were reputed to be one hundred per cent on the Nazi side. Here in this southern extremity of the Division's line, the 394th Infantry Regiment was spread out over five miles, covering one of the main roads running from Germany into Belgium and linking up with the 14th Cavalry Group which did a not-too-effective job of screening the gap between the 99th Division and its neighbour, the raw 106th Infantry Division.

Those who had been at West Point knew that the Losheim gap, the narrow valley occupied by Colonel Mark Devine's 14th Cavalry, was one of the classic westward invasion routes. Studied by generations of cadets at St Cyr, Namur, Spandau, Sandhurst and West Point, the seven-mile corridor through the Ardennes had seen the German invasions of 1870, 1914 and 1940. Now it was defended solely by the right flank of the 394th Infantry and Colonel Devine's nine hundred dismounted cavalrymen, located in six fortified hamlets near the frontier with gaps of up to one thousand yards between their positions, through which, it was rumoured, Belgians conscripted into the German Army went home on leave and where a German patrol had recently stolen a Sherman tank and driven it off without discovery.

1st Lieutenant Lyle Bouck, dug in on a hill outside the village of Lanzerath, was worried. Bouck, of the 39th Regiment's Intelligence and Recce Platoon, had been hearing unusual noises to his front for a day and a half. Bouck had been six years in the Army and he did not share the easy-going attitude of the officers from a section of the 14th Cavalry's tank destroyers who were located to his front in the village of Lanzerath itself. On the 15th, he had had his men on duty all night. Now most of them were asleep; yet Bouck himself could not sleep; there was something in the wind, but he did not know what.

In the village of Krewinkel, Sergeant Bannister of Lieutenant Farrens' platoon of the 14th Cavalry was also worried. But he had more evidence to justify his forebodings. Twice before dawn he got up from his sleeping-bag and stared out of the window of the little Belgian house in which he was billeted. The day before, he had spotted half a company of German infantry dragging a heavily-laden sledge to a house in his section of the line. He had not been able to work out what was on the sledge, but it worried him.

But if here and there the men in the line worried about what the morrow would bring, the High Command was satisfied that 16 December, 1944, would be exactly the same as the preceding day. General Hodges, of the First Army, who was in charge of the Ardennes, was unconcerned about the 'ghost front'; he was preoccupied with the 2nd Division attack on the Roer dams, which was vitally important to his future strategy. Admittedly, back at his headquarters in the Hotel Britannica in the Belgian resort town of Spa, his pessimistically-inclined intelligence chief, Colonel 'Monk' Dickson, had predicted on the 15th that, 'although the enemy is resorting to his attack propaganda to bolster morale of the troops it is possible that a limited scale offensive will be launched for the purpose of achieving a Christmas morale "victory" for civilian consumption'. But presumably the colonel did not take his prediction too seriously for on the same day he left for Paris, with the blessing of General Hodges, to take his first four-day leave since the 1st Army had landed in Normandy six months earlier.

Further to the rear at the Hotel Alpha, Luxemburg, General

Omar Bradley, the commander of 12th Army Group, was equally unconcerned. A few days before he had said to the press, 'If the other fellow only would hit us now! We could kill more Germans with a good deal less effort if they'd only climb out of their holes and come after us for a change'. Now, just prior to dawn on the sixteenth, he was preparing himself for the long drive from Luxemburg City to Supreme Commander's HQ at Versailles, to discuss the replacement problem, especially of riflemen, which was becoming acute after the heavy losses of the previous month.

At Versailles itself, the mood was one of supreme confidence. The Germans were finished. Two Flying Fortresses, equipped with special radio equipment, were ready for the moment when Berlin fell to act as mobile communications centres.

Thus the 75,000 men of the US 1st Army slept towards a dawn, which would bring a day just like the previous one—cold, dreary and uncomfortable but nonetheless safe. They did not hear the muffled tramp of a quarter of a million German troops moving up into the line opposite them. Nor did they hear the small pre-dawn noises of the German tankers getting their Panzers ready for the moment when their engines must burst into life. They did not sense the 2,000 cannon of all sizes pointing in their direction, with their gun-layers already sitting at their pieces, eyes stuck against the rubber-mounted lens, ready to fire, while to their front in the firs the white-clad storm battalions stamped their boots in the pre-dawn cold.

2

At five-thirty a.m. the German guns cracked into action. Far to the rear of the enemy line at the little town of Prüm, a huge railway gun opened the barrage. It was followed by hundreds of other guns of all calibres. From his observation post on the hill outside Lanzerath, Lieutnant Bouck watched horrified as the whole horizon erupted in a violent crackle of yellow and red explosions. Diving for their foxholes, his little platoon buried their heads desperately in the bottoms of the frozen trenches.

Every American position in the Losheim Gap was struck by the tremendous artillery barrage. Frantically, soldiers and civilians, rudely awakened from their sleep, grabbed their weapons and fled to the cellars and strongpoints dug into the flinty soil of the hillsides. At the 14th Cavalry headquarters at Manderfeld, officers grabbed the phones and started bellowing orders. Messengers ran to their vehicles. Motors coughed and spluttered. And still the shells kept coming down. From both sides of the Gap, from the 106th Infantry Division and its neighbour the 99th, the reports started to flood in alarmingly.

5.50 A.M.—from 423rd, 106th Division: ANTI-TANK CO. SHELLED BY ARTILLERY SINCE 5.30.

6.23 A.M.—from 99th Infantry Division: DIVISION TAKING HEAVY SHELLING ALL ALONG SECTOR . . .

For one long hour it went on. Then as abruptly as it had started, the shelling stopped. *What the hell was going on?* They came out of their foxholes, weapons gripped tightly in sweaty hands, and stared anxiously to their front, trying to penetrate the thick fog that had rolled in from the hills.

The Germans came without any attempt at concealment. Three divisions, their forward elements coming out of the hills in their thousands, tramped down to the American positions as if they were on parade or as if they disdained the puny efforts of the defenders to stop them.

Sergeant John Bannister saw the Germans through a window, marching down the road four and five abreast, whistling and singing as if there were no Americans within miles. 'Perhaps they don't know we're here', he thought, 'Or perhaps they're just too damned over-confident'.

Quickly his squad positioned its machine-guns in the second floor of the house and waited till the Germans came within twenty yards of the barbed wire fence the platoon had thrown around the village. Then they opened up with everything they had. The first ranks of the Germans withered away. Their bodies flew to all sides and the air was filled with the cries of rage and bewilderment. But they came again. A squad broke off from the main body, ran forward and tried to breach the wire. There was a short series of explosions that ripped their bodies apart. They had run into the booby traps the cavalrymen had planted there.

Another group of three, covered by two riflemen, doubled to the right and set up their mortars. Swiftly they began to lob their bombs into the American positions and while the defenders cowered on the littered floor of the house, fifty Germans entered the village. But the Americans were in an ideal defensive position from which they could completely cover the snowy ridge the Germans had to cross.

Soon after dawn they gave up—for the time being. A retreating German, pausing in his flight to the rear, cupped his hand around his mouth and cried in rage. 'Take a ten-minute break, soldier. We'll be back!' To which, Bannister's boss Lieutenant Farrens yelled back 'Yeah, and we'll be waiting for you—you son of a bitch!'

One hour later it was reported from the first of the 14th Cavalry's fortified hamlets, Roth, that the enemy was in the village and that a tank some seventy-five yards away was 'belting us with direct fire'. Hurriedly Colonel Devine sent light tanks to help the defenders, but they didn't get far before shells from a battery of 88s brought them to an abrupt halt.

Roth held out for two more hours. Then Captain Stanley Porche, C.O. of the Roth position, radioed his nearest neighbour, Lieutenant Herdrich, at Kobscheid, and told him 'We're moving back! Your friends to the south are moving back too [the 106th Infantry Division]. It's up to you whether you withdraw on foot or in vehicles. I advise you to go on foot'. Porche and his men never made it; they were taken prisoner two hours later.

Herdrich decided to fight on. Private Sklepkowski of his

mortar squad grabbed some fast-fused booby-trap grenades and began to lob them at the advancing Germans through a slit in the wall of Herdrich's C.P. They exploded at chest height, creating fearful wounds, and stopped the German attack almost at once. The enemy broke and ran.

Up to now Lt Bouck had not been attacked. Ten minutes after the bombardment had ended, he saw that the 14th Cavalry tank destroyers in Lanzerath were pulling out of the rear. He called regimental headquarters and asked for instructions. He was told to send a patrol down to Lanzerath and find out what was going on in the village. He picked three men and, with himself in the lead, made a careful approach to the empty village. Furtively he neared the house that had been used by the tank destroyers as their observation post. The door was swinging open, evidence of the hasty retreat of the cavalrymen. He peered over the edge of the ditch in which he and his three men were hiding. No sign of the enemy. He'd risk it. Gripping his carbine more firmly, he signalled them to get up and rush the house.

They clattered up the stone-flagged path, into the ground floor, strewn with abandoned bits and pieces of US equipment, and up the stairs to the bedroom, from where they could look out towards the German lines. As Bouck swung through the door. He stopped dead. A large heavily-built man in civilian clothes was sitting facing the window and speaking in German over the public telephone line! Private Tsakainkas, known as Sak was first to react. He was the most aggressive man in the platoon. Pulling out his bayonet, he cried 'Reach!' The civilian did not understand English, but he understood the gesture well enough and raised his hands. Bouck did some quick thinking. He knew that the population of the area was predominantly pro-German. Prior to 1919 they had been German anyhow, and when the Germans had come back in 1940 over 8,000 of them had enlisted in the German Army. Those who had remained behind were, in the opinion of the average G.I., nothing better than spies, feeding information to the German intelligence men who had roamed the area freely prior to the battle. If this man were a spy he ought to be killed on the spot. But what if the Germans attacked while he was still trapped in the village? It wouldn't look too good.

Making a quick decision, he snapped, 'Let him go'. Sak indicated the street with a jerk of his head and the civilian fled, grinning all over.

Bouck dismissed the man from his thoughts. Out of the window he could see what looked like hundreds of Germans massing to his front, and they were coming in his direction. 'Sak,' he said, 'you come with me. Robinson,' he turned to the oldest man in his platoon, 'you and Creger stay here and observe down the road. As soon as that Kraut column comes into the home stretch, about a mile down the way, come back up to the platoon.' Then he and his runner made their way back to the platoon positions and tried to telephone the regiment. The lines were out. He tried the radio and got through. But the officer at the other end would not believe his report of the massed German formations. 'Damn it,' Bouck bellowed, 'Dont tell me what I don't see! I have twenty-twenty vision. Bring down some artillery, all the artillery you can on the road south of Lanzerath. There's a Kraut column coming up from that direction!'

But he waited in vain. No artillery came. Yet Bouck had no time to consider why. Almost immediately Robinson came on the field phone, using wire left behind by the retreating cavalry-men. 'The Krauts are already downstairs! What shall we do?'

By noon every one of the key villages in the seven mile Gap was either taken, under severe attack or about to be attacked. The roads in and out of the area were jammed with traffic, some going up to the front, but most of it hurrying to the rear.

At Manderfeld everthing was confusion. Mortar shells were already falling on the outskirts. The main street was packed with men 'bugging out' and terrified civilians who had sided with the Americans and wanted to get out before they suffered the vengeance they expected the well-informed Germans to inflict upon them. In the headquarters itself, the staff was packing documents prior to abandoning the CP. A little while earlier Colonel Devine had said emphatically 'We will stay here'; now he was beginning to lose his nerve.

At 1100 he ordered a general withdrawal. It was to be the first of his withdrawal orders that day, most of them without permission from higher headquarters, which would end in his being relieved of his command and in an Inspector-General's investigation of his organisation's conduct during the opening stages of the battle.

At Kobscheid, Herdrich found himself surrounded on all sides, his escape route to the rear cut off. But he did not surrender. Destroying their heavy equipment, the members of his platoon slipped into the gloomy fir forests in threes and fours and started on their three-day escape to their own lines.

At Krewinkel, Bannister's platoon, with their ammunition running out, loaded up into their three armoured cars and five jeeps and made a run for it. As they left, white-clad German infantry started to come out of the forests on all sides. They made it, only to be jeered at as cowards by reinforcements coming up from the west as their little convoy rolled through Manderfeld.

But even the reinforcements did not stay long. By early afternoon individual buildings were burning in Manderfeld. The roads to the rear were packed with fleeing men and vehicles. Here and there there were already signs of the breakdown in morale. Men had thrown away their weapons; some had even torn off their helmets and the rest of their military gear, while others sat apathetically on top of the hastily-laden vehicles, their faces buried in their hands. Soon Colonel Devine and most of his staff would depart to the rear, never to return.

In the villages now abandoned by the Americans and soon to be occupied yet again by the triumphant Germans at their heels, the villagers began the task of clearing away the traces of American occupancy. The Stars and Stripes, the pictures of

Roosevelt and Churchill, the myriad bits and pieces of US equipment were tossed through the windows into the cobbled streets. '*Unsere Jungs kommen wieder!*'[1] they called to each other.

3

The Germans hit Lieutenant Bouck's positions as they were on a routine march. They came in two columns, marching on both sides of the road from Lanzerath, arms slung, tightly packed together, unconcerned that there might be the enemy waiting for them.

Bouck, who had spent two years as an instructor at Fort Benning, recognised them as paratroopers from their long, shapeless camouflaged smocks and rimless helmets. Immediately he reported the information and considered what to do. There were several hundred Germans and he had sixteen men under his command, though admittedly he was well-armed and in a very good defensive position. Should he open fire on them now? He decided to wait for the main body, and watched as the German paratroopers filed behind his positions, taking the right fork in the direction of the village of Losheimergraben. Bouck counted them roughly. There seemed to be about three hundred men. Then three separate figures appeared on the road. To Sak, eager as ever to get into action, these three men appeared to be the paratroop commander and his staff. They would be worth shooting. Unknown to Lieutenant Bouck, he lined up his sights on the first man and prepared to fire. Just at that moment, a little girl ran out of a nearby house. He hesitated. If he fired now, he might hit her too.[2]

Then it was too late. The little girl was obviously a German sympathiser. She took the German by the arm and pointed urgently in the direction of the American positions. The

[1] 'Our boys are coming back again!'
[2] Twenty-three years later in 1967, William James, as 'Sak' calls himself now, was to meet that little girl, Tina Scholzen, who still lives in Lanzerath. Now she is married and has children of her own.

German reacted at once. He shouted something. The para-troopers flung themselves into the ditches at both sides of the road, and immediately the fire fight broke out. It went on all day. Sak was in his element, manning the platoon's ·50 calibre machine-gun, spraying the ditches and the woods beyond. He was determined that no aid would come to the Germans trapped on the road below. Meanwhile Bouck had grabbed the radio and called once again for artillery support. None came. Desperately he called regiment once more. 'What shall we do then?' he demanded. 'Hold it at all costs!' came back the laconic reply. A moment later a slug hit his radio and he lost contact with regiment for good. The last remaining link in the Gap between the 106th Infantry and the 99th Infantry was broken.

At noon the Germans asked for a truce while they evacuated their wounded, lying out in front of Bouck's positions. Keeping a watchful eye on the German first aid men, Bouck agreed. It was a chance to get a rest and have a look at his own position. It wasn't too good. Although casualties were surprisingly light, with only one man seriously wounded, his men were getting tired and worried. They knew that they were surrounded and that regiment was not going to be able to get them out of the mess they were in.

As soon as the last German medic had disappeared down the hill, mortars opened up from below Lanzerath. They landed in heavy plops all around. The Americans grabbed their weapons. The paratroopers were coming up the hill again! Three of them crawled to within shooting distance of Pfc Milosevich, who was protecting the left flank with a ·30 calibre light machine-gun. Sak seized a machine pistol and fired a burst at them. They fell back as if struck by some gigantic metal fist. He could not stop himself firing. With his finger seemingly bound for ever on the trigger of the quivering grease gun, he poured a whole magazine into their dead bodies, turning one of them clean over with the impact.

Towards late afternoon, with the young paratroopers piled in front of his position, Bouck began to think it was time he got his men out. During a lull he called Sak over to him and told him he wanted him to take out the men who wanted to go.

'Are you coming?' Sak asked. 'No, I have orders to hold on at all costs. I'm staying.' 'Then we'll all stay'. Sak replied. Before Bouck had time to argue, the German attack started again. But a little later as it started to get dark, he sent Corporal Jenkins and Private Preston back with orders to bring reinforcements. Neither returned.

Now, as the darkness of the first day of the offensive, which Winston Churchill was soon to name the 'Battle of the Bulge', started to descend, the Germans began to infiltrate the American positions. Abandoning their disastrous rush tactics, they crept from foxhole to foxhole silencing the defenders individually.

A volley of 9 mm bullets from a machine pistol caught Sak in the face. By turning him to one side, Bouck could see the extent of the wound. It was terrifying. His cheek had been shot away with the right eye lying limply in the bloody wound like some grotesque pearl in an oyster shell.

'I'll get you out of here,' Bouck cried, dragging him out of the foxhole where he had fallen. At that moment the Germans were upon him. A German officer, pistol in hand, took one look at Sak's ruined face and cried out in horror. Two others, crazed and weeping with the slaughter of the day, tried to kill the two wounded men, for Bouck had been wounded in the leg. But the German officer thrust himself between them and the Americans, crying out loudly, '*Nein!*'

Supported by another German soldier, the limping Bouck began to carry the barely conscious Sak down the hill to Lanzerath. The long road to the prisoner-of-war camp had begun.

Towards midnight the two American soldiers found themselves sprawled among a mixed group of Germans and American prisoners in the one café that Lanzerath possessed. Against one wall stood the zinc-topped bar, now long empty of the evil-tasting local damson brandy. Against the other a cheap-looking cuckoo clock which had somehow survived four years of looting soldiery, incongruously cuckooed the hours away.

The Germans had finished interrogating their prisoners. Now everyone was trying to get some sleep, save Bouck who was still attempting in vain to staunch the blood which flowed freely from Sak's dreadful wound and stained his field jacket. The atmosphere was thick with male sweat, the stink of the oil used to grease rifles and the stench of the cheap black tobacco used in German cigarettes. Bouck tried to keep his eyes open.

Abruptly the door of the café was flung open. A gust of icy air swept in. With it came a tall lean man, who paused momentarily at the door, seemingly unconcerned at the fact he was allowing the light to escape and give away the position, and stared with undeniable contempt at the scene before him.

Then he banged the door closed and strode across the room to where the colonel of the 9th Parachute Regiment, which had attacked Bouck's position all that day, was resting. Bouck looked at the new arrival with interest. Under the yellow light, he caught a glimpse of the silver sparkle of the runic SS the man wore on the collar of his camouflaged jacket. He was an SS colonel.

4

The young colonel, one of the youngest regimental commanders in the German Army, was Joachim Peiper (he preferred to be called *Jochen*), C.O. of the premier regiment of the premier division of enemy armed forces: the 1st Panzer Regiment of the 1st SS Division, Adolf Hitler's Bodyguard.

Peiper was the son of a regular officer from a traditional military family, and it seemed natural when he graduated from high school in Berlin in 1933 that he should join the Army. His father had visualised him entering the élite 'Cavalry Regiment Number Four' and with this aim in mind had accepted the suggestion of Colonel von Reichenau that Jochen should join the local *SS Reitersturm*. This was a volunteer SS cavalry unit, patronised by Berlin's upper classes and including a couple of princes in its ranks. According to von Reichenau Jochen could learn to ride with the SS and then when he was finished with school could enter the cavalry. His father thought it was a good idea, so Jochen joined.

But when the time came for him to join the cavalry, he was no longer interested. Unlike most of his contemporaries from the older army families, he was only interested in entering the newly-formed 'Black Guards'. So he volunteered for the élite Nazi formation although this meant that, in spite of possessing a high school diploma, he would have to serve some time in the ranks before he could be commissioned. (If he had joined the *Reichswehr*, he would have immediately acquired the rank of officer-cadet because of his education.)

After some initial service in Berlin, he was picked for officer-cadet school and sent to Brunswick, from whence he graduated the following year and was immediately assigned to *Reichsfuehrer* Heinrich Himmler's staff to be one of his adjutants. Here he was regarded as a useful, well-educated officer, who spoke fluent French and English and could add a little tone to the 'upstart SS', as the Black Guards were regarded in Berlin society and in regular army circles.

One day, however, Himmler discovered that his handsome young adjutant was not a member of the Nazi Party. Noting that Peiper did not wear the swastika tie-pin of a party member with his dress uniform, he asked him whether or not he had joined. When Peiper told him that he had not and wasn't going to join now and receive a high party number, Himmler immediately telephoned Martin Bormann and told him that as soon as a low party number became vacant, he would need it for his adjutant. But a low number never became vacant, so Peiper, one day regarded as the epitome of the Nazi soldier, never joined the Party.[1]

---

[1] At this time thousands were joining the Party in order to gain personal and political advantage. A high Party number was therefore regarded as the sign of an opportunist.

On the outbreak of war, Lieutenant Peiper reported at once to the *Leibstandarte*, 'the Adolf Hitler Bodyguard Regiment', where he commanded a company in the campaign in Poland and won the Iron Cross. As a result he was offered command of a battalion when the campaign was over. He was then twenty-five years old and highly regarded as a capable, up-and-coming young officer.

The years passed. There was the campaign in France and later in the Balkans. Peiper fought everywhere, but he only began to show his real talent as a leader of men in Russia in the years 1942–1943 when the steam started to go out of the German *Drang nach Osten*.

In February, 1943, when the Russians had launched a surprise counter-attack over the River Donetz, Peiper was ordered to take his tank battalion and break through to the trapped 320th German Infantry Division, which was trying to fight its way back to the German lines, although hampered by some 1,500 wounded. It was the depths of the Russian winter and the trapped division was over twenty miles away, deep in the heart of the Soviet Army which was enveloping it.

Peiper broke through to the trapped division without meeting any real Russian resistance. Forming a defensive position around the long convoy of ambulances and little horse-drawn carts, he let his men rest for the night before he started the long haul back.

Next morning the slow convoy got underway early, but somehow the Russians had got information about his intentions; partisans were everywhere. A ski battalion had moved up during the night and seized a village that barred the road they were to take. Peiper had no time to plan an elaborate tactical approach. His tanks left the road and encircled the village, coming in from the rear. The fight that followed was sharp but short. The Russians died in their positions or fled the way they had come and the slow-moving column rolled on.

Late that day Peiper's men reached the river. Under the cover of the tanks, two spots were discovered where the ice was thick enough to allow the passage of the ambulances and carts. When the wounded were safely within their own lines, Peiper turned and drove back the way he had come. The ice was too thin for his heavy vehicles. He would have to find a crossing elsewhere. Another commander might have told himself he had done enough already, destroyed his vehicles, and crossed the ice on foot. But Peiper was determined to save his tanks, and he did. A few days later when the Germans went over to the counter-attack it was Major Peiper who captured the two bridgeheads which were decisive for the German plan. No one was surprised when he was awarded Germany's highest decoration—the Knight's Cross—for his exploits that February.

But Peiper was not one of those medal-hunting commanders common to most armies who sacrifice their men's lives to their own ambitions. Peiper did not hesitate to get down among his men and fight with a rifle in his hand like the ordinary soldier when the going got tough. In the summer of 1943 when his position was overrun by Soviet tanks, he grabbed a rifle grenade and a grenade launcher and while the rest of his men thought it more opportune to bury themselves in their foxholes, he waited till a T-34 was within yards of him before he fired the grenade launcher. The Russian tank disappeared in a burst of violent red and yellow flame and when his men lifted their heads shame-facedly from their trenches, all that the grinning Peiper said, was: 'I suppose that should suffice to get me the combat infantryman's badge, eh?'

In November, 1943, he was given the 1st Panzer Regiment of the *Leibstandarte*, a high honour for a man of his age in a division full of brave men with years of combat experience. But one month later Peiper proved that he was worthy of the command. In December, he drove his battle group deep into the enemy lines, broke up the staffs of four Soviet divisions, defeated several Russian units and captured or destroyed 100 tanks and 76 anti-tank guns. The drive, which took him twenty-five miles behind the Russian lines, won him the coveted oak leaves to the Knight's Cross and the reputation of being an officer to be watched as probably the youngest future general of the *Waffen SS*, and a commander not afraid of executing long-range penetrations behind enemy lines, even when he was completely cut off from his base.

But Russia had left its scars on Jochen Peiper, both physical and psychological. His once handsome young face had become hard and ruthless. In those Russian winters he had seen more than his share of death—and in his heart he knew by now that violent death would be the end of his own career. That knowledge and the experiences he had undergone in the artificial life of the front had cut him off from the desires of the normal man for home and family, although he himself was married and had children. The *Leibstandarte* had become the only family he had, and when, as happened time and time again in the severe battles of the Eastern Front that family was wiped out, he found a new one in the innocent-faced eighteen-year-old lads who came streaming to the regiment in their hundreds, as if they were only too eager to pay their tribute to the Hitler ideal in their own blood.

By 1944, the young colonel, as he was now, was a harsh, ruthless, sometimes arrogant officer, though unlike so many of his colleagues he had the saving grace, in Anglo-Saxon eyes at least, of having a pleasant sense of humour.[1] By the fifth year of combat his personality had hardened into that particular German combination of naïve, almost boyish idealism linked to the savage spirit of a brutal soldier of fortune who knows only one real loyalty. Not to God, not to his country, not even to his family—but to his own unit, the *Leibstandarte Adolf Hitler*.

The *Leibstandarte Adolf Hitler* had begun its career as a unit in 1933 when Hitler, who was terrified of plots against his life, ordered a special bodyguard to be formed to protect him after

[1] It sometimes took macabre, almost suicidal, forms. After three 'starts' he took up an aeroplane accompanied by a scared company doctor 'because I'll be needing you immediately if anything happens'. Another time he thoroughly scared the wits out of a pompous party official who didn't believe Peiper's statement that there were partisans in the area by blowing up the man's front door during the night. After that the man believed him.

the Berlin *Reichstag* was burned down in that year. He gave the job of commanding the bodyguard to his old party comrade and former chauffeur, Sepp Dietrich. The burly Bavarian set about forming the unit with his usual energy, selecting 120 men, all over six foot, who formed a triple cordon around Hitler at the *Reichskanzelei*, through which every visitor to the dictator must pass. They also served his meals, wearing neat white jackets above their black trousers, fumbling a little and awkward in their new role as waiters. And when Hitler ventured out his great black Horch was always filled with alert-eyed, heavily-armed, black-clad giants.

After the *Reichskanzelei* was rebuilt to Hitler's taste a year later, they also took over the guard of the front portal from the soldiers of the regular army. Soon the photographs and news-reels of the two black-clad giants, with their white cross-straps and highly polished rifles, became familiar to people all over the world. To many they also symbolised the brutal efficiency of the new régime in Germany.

In September, 1933, at the Nuremberg Party Rally, Hitler gave his new bodyguard, which up to this time had been called the 'staff guard', its new name—*SS Leibstandarte Adolf Hitler*. And two months later on November 9, the tenth anniversary of the abortive Munich Putsch, the *Leibstandarte* was sworn in by a special oath which bound them unconditionally, body and soul to the person of Adolf Hitler. At the time the new oath escaped the attention of most Germans. The ceremony had been impressive and the young giants of the *Leibstandarte* had been excellently turned out. That was all. What they didn't realise was that Hitler had created a new praetorian guard, as in ancient Rome, which owed its loyalty not to the state, but to the ruler of that state.

But Sepp Dietrich, although he had served as a sergeant in the old Bavarian Army from 1911 to 1918, knew little of modern warfare. Undoubtedly he possessed toughness, bravery and moral courage, which made him very popular with his men, but he was no commander. As one of his war time corps commanders, General Bittrich, was to say of him: 'I once spent an hour and a half trying to explain a situation to Sepp Dietrich with the aid of a map. It was quite useless. He understood nothing at all.' Goering said of him: 'He had at the most the ability to command a division'; and Rundstedt summed him up as: 'Decent and stupid'. Thus it was that the training of the *Leibstandarte* was placed in the hands of the 9th Infantry Regiment, which had once supplied the guards for the *Reichskanzelei*.

But if Dietrich allowed the army to train his men, he still retained a strictly personal, independent control of his special unit. So much so that in 1935, Himmler, the head of the SS, wrote to him: 'My dear Sepp, This is of course another impossibility. Your officers are good enough to recognise me personally. Otherwise the *Leibstandarte* is a law to itself. It does anything it likes without taking the slightest notice of orders from above.'

In this manner the *Leibstandarte* quickly developed into a rough, tough, intensely parochial outfit, ready to brawl with Wehrmacht soldiers or even men of other SS units at the drop of a hat, their loyalty strictly limited to their own officers and their own comrades.

As the thirties drew to a close and the war approached, the *Leibstandarte* began to grow to regimental strength. But still it insisted on getting the cream of Germany's eligible youth. Naturally all the members of the *Leibstandarte* were volunteers —and there were volunteers enough from the fanatical, well-indoctrinated young men who had passed through the Hitler Youth and the *Arbeitsdienst*. But the entrance regulations were stringent. Firstly the recruit, who had to be between seventeen and twenty-two, had to prove he was untainted by Jewish blood from 1760 onwards. Secondly he had to be over 6 feet 0·5 inches in height, and in perfect physical condition—even a single filling in a tooth disqualified him. And thirdly, if he wished to become an officer, he had to be prepared to serve two years in the ranks, though in contrast to the regular army, the *Leibstandarte* did not demand that its officer candidates should have a secondary school leaving qualification.

These latter officer cadets were the élite within an élite. After their two years in the ranks, where they developed a much closer relationship with the men than officers in the army did, they went either to the *SS Junkerschule* at Bad Tölz or to the *SS Junkerschule* at Braunschweig. Both these cadet schools were harsh, brutal places, where a high premium was placed on top physical fitness and endurance in adversity. Training, too, was much more realistic than in the regular army, with a great deal of live ammunition being used. As war drew closer, for instance, the young officers-to-be were given shovels and told to dig one-man holes. When they had completed these within a given time, a platoon of tanks were driven over the positions. It was just too bad for the man who had not dug his hole deep enough. It is also recorded that cadets were given a grenade to place on their helmets. When it was safely balanced there, they were told by their instructor, who had withdrawn to a safe distance, to pull the pin and stand to attention until the grenade exploded. Usually there was no damage done if the cadet kept rigidly still and let the explosion dissipate itself above his steel-clad head. However, if he got rattled and let the grenade fall . . .

By 1939 the *Leibstandarte* had made up for what it lacked in military tradition by its enthusiasm and fanatical devotion to its own flag. Already it was well on the way to becoming that élite unit, comparable to the British Guards, the American Leather-necks—or perhaps, better the French Paras of the post-war period, which had surrounded itself by an aura of swaggering toughness and hard masculinity. Inspired by the feeling that it was an aristocratic minority, superior to the general run of other soldiers, and cut off from them by its own special rules and loyalties, the *Leibstandarte* set out to become master of the battlefield.

The *Leibstandarte* was blooded as an armoured infantry regiment in the campaign in Poland, suffering higher casualties than any of the other regular army units in the corps to which it was attached. Losses among the officers were especially high. Pulled out in the period of the *Sitzkrieg* which followed, the *Leibstandarte* was refitted and built up to the strength of a reinforced regiment for its next assignment, the attack on neutral Holland. After a spectacular dash of seventy miles in one day, the regiment managed to get in at the last of the fighting around Rotterdam, where one group achieved a kind of fame by seriously wounding General Student, the German airborne commander, two hours after the cease-fire had taken place.

From Holland the *Leibstandarte* went to France and from France to Russia, after a high-speed jaunt into Greece. It was in Russia that the *Leibstandarte*, now an armoured division, really came into its own. In those first years of the campaign, the Division was everywhere, at the head of every advance, at the rear of every withdrawal, fighting desperately, boldly and sometimes spectacularly, the hope of every German commander and the fear of every Russian one on whose front it appeared. It seized a vital bridgehead across the Dneiper. It broke through the Russian defences in the Crimea. It stormed Rostov. It recaptured Charkov. It tried to break through to the beleagured 6th Army in Stalingrad. Those long-drawn-out battles for obscure villages in the snowy wastes of the Soviet Union broke many an élite German regular army unit, and not a few commanders in those terrible winters of '42 and '43 preferred to reach for their pistols rather than face up once again to the task of building a new unit from a shattered handful of exhausted grey-faced skeletons who had once been members of a proud regiment.

Not so the *Leibstandarte*. Those winter campaigns hardened it and transformed it into a unit which did not seem to understand the meaning of failure. But playing the role of the 'Fuehrer's Firebrigade', rushed from one front to another, wherever there was an emergency—a fire that only the *Leibstandarte* could put out—entailed severe casualties. And by late '43, the number one SS division was accepting entries into its hallowed Germanic ranks from a dozen European countries, including even the decadent enemy of two years before, France.

From all over Europe they came, the naïve, crooked, enthusiastic, turncoat youths, believing in the lies of the recruiting posters displayed in their dead European towns. For them the silver SS symbol simply meant high adventure and glory, fighting for 'a united Europe against the Soviet sub-human'. In the training units, the 'Germanic' and the 'Greater Germany' concepts were played down. Now that the Germans were fighting with their backs to the wall in Russia, the 'European concept' became the motto of the day. Bad Tölz trained future SS officers from such varied countries as Norway and Lithuania. Dutch SS officers taught German cadets. A Belgian, Leo Degrelle, became the commander of an SS regiment and won the Knight's Cross. It was even suggested that British and American POWs should be invited to take part in SS training courses so that they too would be infected by the heady new European idea.

But these eager 'volunteers' brought with them a different ethos from the older SS men. They had swallowed the preposterous anti-Soviet propaganda of their teachers without question. They did not know the reality of the Russian front. For them the Russians were mongrel sub-humans to be 'liquidated' (a favourite word) without a passing thought, as were the members of any other nation that stood in the way of fulfilling their 'Mission'. Combined with the older SS men who had already been brutalised by two years of war in the inhuman conditions of the Russian front, they formed groups characterised by swift, often pointless, savagery.

Atrocities had certainly been committed by the SS before the 'volunteers' had appeared in any number. In 1940, for instance, when a hundred men of the 2nd Norfolk Regiment had refused to surrender at Le Paradis during the retreat to Dunkirk, the men of the SS Regiment *Totenkopf* had massacred the ones who survived after the resultant battle. The massacre caused a mild sensation within the ranks of the German Army and the commander of the unit responsible was threatened with a court martial.[1] Two years later the *Leibstandarte* itself took severe measures when it discovered that six of its men captured by the Russians had been murdered by the GPU. For three days they took no Russian prisoners and one German colonel estimated that 10,000 Russians were shot during that period.

Once the 'volunteers' started to flood into the SS, the number of 'incidents' rose rapidly. In Italy there were mass executions at Boves, south of Cuneo, in reprisal for partisan attacks on German soldiers. In the village of Oradour-sur-Glane, in South-West France, SS men destroyed every house and shot most of the population after the Maquis had shot one of the unit's officers. In Normandy an SS regiment shot 64 British and Canadian prisoners. The catalogue of such incidents could be continued *ad nauseam*.

The *Waffen SS* had become Europe's scourge: a ruthless, heartless collection of first-class soldiers, fighting for an idea which had long since lost its validity and a glory that had vanished years before. And among all the many SS units formed by the end of 1944, there was none more battle-hardened, more brutalised and more ruthless than the premier division of the whole corps—the *1 SS-Panzerdivision 'Leibstandarte Adolf Hitler'*.

5

In December, 1944, the *Leibstandarte* was given a task greater than any it had received throughout the war. It was to lead a new offensive in the West which would smash the Anglo-American armies and change the course of the whole war.

As a member of the 6th SS Panzer Army, commanded by Dietrich, it was to break through the thinly-held American line on a front from Rötgen to Losheim, part of a nine-division force. In front of it, two infantry divisions, the 3rd Parachute and the 12th Volksgrenadier, were to break a hole through the

[1] He was finally court-martialled and hanged by the British in 1948.

American line in the Losheim Gap into which would pour the 1 SS, led by General Mohnke. The division would then advance rapidly to the River Meuse and capture bridges in the Huy area. From there the advance of the four SS panzer divisions in the Sixth Army would continue to Antwerp, the main Allied supply port on the Continent of Europe. The strategic and political aims of this daring new offensive were to divide the British and American armies, capture their main source of supplies and frustrate Britain's ability to continue the war in Europe. Even if this latter objective were not achieved, the war would definitely be extended and Hitler confidently expected that the Anglo-American-Soviet coalition would then break down. As a result, although he might not win the war, he would definitely achieve a better peace than that of 'unconditional surrender', which was the current Allied aim.

But Hitler was determined that the great victory he expected to achieve in the West must be achieved by his *own* army—the men of the Waffen SS, who had not betrayed him like those of the regular Wehrmacht, which had revolted against him in July. The SS must be given the best arms, the best tanks, the best equipment; they must give him victory, and at their head must be *his* division, the one which bore his own name—the *Leibstandarte Adolf Hitler*.

The man who was to lead the *Leibstandarte's* drive to the bridges of the Meuse was Jochen Peiper. With a strong battle group made of some 5,000 men, spread over Tiger, Panther and Royal Tiger units, plus mobile flak, self-propelled guns and engineers, with the addition of a battalion of armoured infantry, Peiper was to go into action as soon as the 12th and 3rd Divisions had made the initial breakthrough.

The route he was to take from the point of breakthrough would lead him west through the village of Honsfeld and on to Baugnez. Here he would turn off in the direction of Ligneuville, from where he would head for the town of Stavelot on the River Amblève, the first of the water barriers he would have to cross. From Stavelot he would continue to the village of Trois

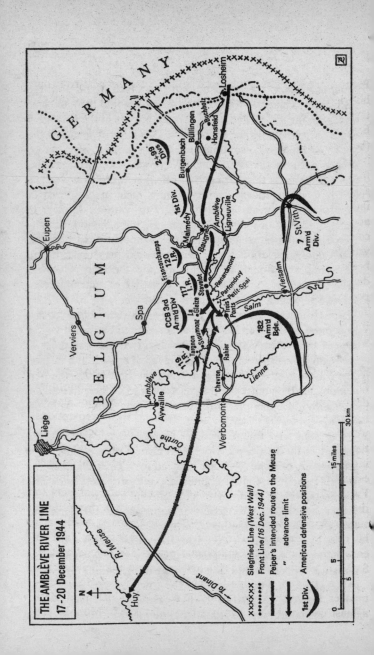

THE AMBLÈVE RIVER LINE
17-20 December 1944

R. Meuse

N

GERMANY

BELGIUM

Liège

Huy

to Dinant

Eupen

Verviers

Spa

Amblève

Aywaille

Ourthe

Werbomont

Chevron

Rahier

Lienne

R. Salm

Vielsalm

St.Vith

7 St.Armd
Div.

182
Armd
Bde.

Trois
Ponts

Petit-Spai

Parfondruy

Renardmont

Stavelot

Trois Ponts

Gleize

La Gleize

Stoumont

Targnon

11 I.R.

CCB 3rd
Armd Div

117
I.R.

120
I.R.

Francorchamps

Malmédy

Baugnez

Amblève

Ligneuville

1st Div.

Burgenbach

Bullingen

Büchholz

Honsfeld

2 + 99
Div.

Losheim

xxxxxxx   Siegfried Line (West Wall)
●●●●●●●   Front Line (16 Dec. 1944)
           Peiper's intended route to the Meuse
    "   advance limit
           American defensive positions
1st Div.

0   5   15 miles
0   5   30 km

Ponts, a vital location, where he would cross the next river on his route, the Salm. Once across the Salm, he would head out of the tight awkward valleys of the Ardennes to Werbomont, where he would join a good motor road along which he would dash to the Meuse.

When Peiper studied the minutely detailed map, which dated from the successful 1940 invasion along the same route, he snorted to his divisional commander, Mohnke, that it was intended 'not for tanks, but bicycles'. Admittedly it had the advantage that the route did not cross too many bridges which could be blown and thus delay his drive, but in most places it was terribly narrow and full of bends, in some places, especially between Ligneuville and Stavelot, it was both these things, and damnably steep as well. But in all cases, it was virtually impossible to move tanks, in particular his gigantic 72-ton Royal Tigers, at any speed; and he knew that speed was of the essence if he were to take advantage of the initial shock among the *Amis* when the surprise offensive hit them.

The more he thought about the road assigned to him the less he liked it. The schedule for the drive to the Meuse, set by Dietrich, was one day for breakthrough and penetration, one day to get the armour through the Ardennes, and one day to reach the river. On the evening of the third day, preparations would begin for the crossing of the Meuse, with bridgeheads on the other side secured by the fourth day. Peiper thought it impossible to keep to this schedule, but his protests fell on deaf ears. He was told the route had been selected for him by the Fuehrer himself and he'd better keep to it if he did not want to risk his head. Peiper, knowing when he was beaten, dropped the subject and contented himself with intensive map work with his officers and a night drive of over fifty miles in a Tiger to ensure that the ground could be covered in the time allocated. Satisfied that it could, he began to concentrate on other matters.

At a briefing on 14 December, with his Corps Commander, Hermann Priess, who had successfully defended Metz against General Patton for over two months, and Mohnke, his divisional commander, both generals had emphasised that he need not bother about his flanks. His objective was the Meuse; he was not to bother about local resistance or stop to mop it up. Peiper, understanding the requirement fully and trained in Guderian's doctrines of rapid armoured advance, was quite prepared to let the follow-up infantry deal with the problems of local resistance or threats to his flanks.

However, the day after the conference he heard that two trainloads of gasoline intended for the Corps had not yet arrived. This meant that he would not have his full ration of fuel. Although he had instructions to take the speediest route to the west and not stop anywhere unnecessarily he would have to stop somewhere to find fuel. How would he get to the Meuse otherwise? Intelligence, which was well supplied with news from spies and German sympathisers on the American side of the line, had informed him that the *Amis* probably had fuel dumps at Büllingen, Stavelot and Spa. Accordingly these three places, north of the axis of advance, were vitally important for him. But he kept to himself this intended diversion to capture fuel.

As the day of the offensive grew nearer, Peiper experienced ever greater doubts about the success of the operation. He saw again in his mind's eye *die Bewegungskarte*—'the movements' map'—with the blue arrows symbolising the U.S. units in the Ardennes. How the devil was he supposed to fight his way through them with one lone battle group? Then he remembered the destruction at Düren, to which his regiment had been sent a few days before to help the local authorities clear up after an Allied air-raid on what was obviously a non-military target. They had almost to 'scrape the bodies' of the dead off the walls and he had felt ready 'to castrate the swine who did this with a broken glass bottle'. It strengthened his resolution to carry out the operation as best he could. Kraemer, too, must have shared his misgivings about the success of the operation; just before it was due to start he called Peiper to his office and told him, 'I don't care how and what you do. Just make it to the Meuse. Even if you've only one tank left when you get there. *The Meuse with one tank—that's all I ask of you ...*' To Peiper the statement could only mean one thing; Kraemer did not believe that Antwerp could be reached. He merely wanted to satisfy the Fuehrer that they had carried out his instructions and had reached the Meuse—that would be an achievement in itself.

December 15 had brought the bad news about the missing supply trains. It had been a blow for Peiper. But the first day of the great offensive was even worse; everything seemed to go wrong. The infantry on both flanks had failed to achieve their objectives in time. Although the 3rd Parachute Division had earned a good reputation in France and it was better equipped and armed than any other infantry division in the Sixth Army, its officers were poor quality and its men green. Now a great confused jam of armoured vehicles was building up in the mud and snow of the road leading into the Losheim Gap, waiting for the signal to advance. Then at midday an urgent signal came through from Corps. 'Turn west to Lanzerath. Third Parachute Division has been stopped. Take over and get them moving again.'

Peiper needed no urging and the first tank soon moved off. The road in front was clogged with the vehicles of the infantry divisions attacking to his front. On both sides of the road the pitiful, slow procession of the walking wounded were toiling back to the aid posts. Suddenly a train of horse-drawn artillery loomed up to his front. Peiper did not hesitate. He rode straight through it, leaving behind plunging horses, cursing drivers and several wagons hanging precariously over the edges of the ditches on both sides of the road.

Now they were getting closer to the scene of the fighting. Above the line of dark firs to the front, there were soft puffs of smoke with yellow flashes at their centre. Both sides of the road were littered with abandoned equipment, American and German. An *Ami* half-track was burning steadily in the sodden field to their right.

Suddenly the column halted. Peiper jumped out of his jeep behind the lead tanks and ran to see what the cause of the trouble was. A Panther was slewed across the road at an awkward angle, a track gone and the driver sitting on its deck holding a bleeding head. 'Mines, sir,' the commander reported. Peiper nodded, taking in the situation. The paratroops had failed to clear the road! They had run over one of their own mines. His combat engineers were far to the rear. It would take an hour at least before he could get them up to the front of the column with their mine detectors. Peiper hesitated for a moment, then he snapped. 'Clear the road by rolling over the mines!', he ordered and turned back to his own vehicle before the tank commander could argue.

The column set off again, its progress marked by periodic explosions as yet another tank or half-track hit a mine. This little stretch of country cost Peiper six armoured vehicles, but in the end he was through the minefield and rattling westwards again.

By midnight he was approaching Lanzerath and the column began to slow down. The one and only street was littered with the rubble of the day's fighting, against which his vehicles bumped in the darkness. Peiper's rage increased. Where the hell were the paratroopers? No sentries. No guides. Nothing.

Then one of his men called to him in the dark. 'They've got their CP over here, sir.' His jeep pulled up in front of the blacked-out café which served as the CP of the 9th Parachute Regiment. Stiffly Peiper clambered out and dropped on to the muddy cobbles.

He felt exhausted but he remembered Kraemer's injunction about 'one tank on the Meuse'.

He opened the door and walked into the café.

Day Two:

SUNDAY, 17 DECEMBER, 1944

'Drive hard, Peiper, and hold the reins loose,'

General Kraemer, Chief-of-Staff,
6th SS Panzer Army.

Peiper looked round the ill-lit café, then at the paratroop colonel. The man looked a typical *Etappenhengst*—a 'rear echelon stallion'—and his unit looked as 'if it had gone to bed instead of waging war'. He was angry. The failure of the 3rd Parachute Division, to which the Colonel's regiment belonged, had thrown the whole time-table off-balance. If they had punched a hole through the Allied line on schedule, he might well have been sitting on the Meuse by now instead of in this miserable Belgian café.

Without considering the fact that the paratroop colonel was higher in rank than he, Peiper pressed him for information, questioning him as if he were a private and not a regimental commander. What was the situation to his front? Were there any more *Amis* in the woods beyond Lanzerath? Why wasn't his regiment moving forward more quickly?

The colonel was full of excuses and apologies. There were Americans everywhere . . . the village of Lanzerath was heavily fortified, with frontal defences made up of mines and pillboxes . . . tanks had also been heard to the rear . . . it was impossible for the Ninth Parachute to attack successfully under such circumstances without armour.

'Have you personally reconnoitered the *Ami* positions in the woods?' Peiper asked.

The colonel hesitated. No, he hadn't. Peiper knew from experience how young soldiers sent on patrol to find out about enemy positions would agree among themselves that the positions were heavily defended even if they'd been no nearer to them than a kilometre. Without asking permission, he took the field telephone and called the commander of the battalion dug in opposite Lanzerath. The man admitted he had received his information on the state of the American defences from one of his captains. The captain was called. He, too, had not personally seen the *Ami* positions. He had got the information from one of his subordinates. Peiper crashed the phone down in a rage. Quickly he ordered the frightened paratrooper to supply him with his leading battalion. He would take the outfit into battle on his tanks. Placing two captured Shermans in front to fool the *Amis*, he followed up with the paratroopers and a mixed bag of Tigers, Panthers and half-tracks filled with his own panzer grenadiers, who would take over the infantry role if, as was most likely, the paratroopers failed. He would kick off the attack by striking at Buchholz Station at precisely 0400. 'Did the Colonel understand?'

The Colonel did. All at once the lazy little café was galvanised into frantic activity. They were going to attack.

At just after 0400, US vehicles were edging slowly forward, bumper to bumper, through the little village of Honsfeld to the rear of Buchholz. They were the survivors of yesterday's battle, trying desperately to escape. Artillery pieces, jeeps, ammunition-carriers, kitchen-trucks, half-tracks filled with tired cavalrymen and frightened cooks—they ground along in first gear in the 'great bug-out', as the GIs were beginning to call the retreat.

Behind the last of these vehicles, a soldier in an unidentifiable uniform suddenly appeared in the middle of the road. He held a darkened flashlight in his hand. Swinging it a couple of times, apparently in some form of signal, he peered to his rear. Then they were there. Two dark shapes, slightly outlined against the night sky by the flickering of the heavy guns to the rear. The man with the flashlight began to walk slowly and carefully towards the village of Honsfeld, a hundred yards or so behind the last American vehicle. To his rear the Shermans rolled forward, their gunners sitting tensely over their pieces, their commanders still standing at their turrets, ready to batten down their hatches in an instant and begin the battle which must come. Behind them, riding with Diefenthal in a Volkswagen jeep came Peiper, angry and disgusted that he had spent so much time planning the attack on Buchholz Station only to find it completely undefended. Now he intended to take Honsfeld by stealth. In three or four hours it would be dawn and he had no more time to waste on these silly little villages.

In Honsfeld, Lieutenant Robert Reppa of the 'Black Horse' troop, whose men had jeered Bannister's survivors from the Krewinkel fight the day before, lay in a hard chair trying to get some sleep. Outside the retreating traffic rumbled by. It was some time before he noticed the change. The sound was unmistakably different. Sitting up suddenly in the hard chair, he said to his first sergeant, William Lovelock, 'They don't sound like ours!'

He hurried to the door and flung it open. A long line of vehicles was grinding by, as they had been all night. But these were different. He spotted a half-track that was certainly no White, the standard vehicle used in the U.S. Army, then a huge tank, twice the size of the American Sherman. 'My God,' he muttered and closed the door quickly. *They were German!*

He turned to the First Sergeant and asked angrily. 'Why didn't Creel warn us?' Creel was the man he had put in charge of a roadblock south of the town. The next moment Creel himself entered the house. 'I was in my armoured car,' the Sergeant explained. 'A guy came walking down the road in front of a big vehicle, swinging a flashlight. Biggest damn tank I've ever seen. With a swastica on it.' 'Well, why the hell didn't you shoot?' 'I figured it'd be best to warn everyone. So here I am.'

Reppa did not stop to argue. He realized that he would be trapped if he didn't get out immediately. 'Get the men ready,' he ordered. 'We're moving out of here. It's dark and we'll just pull into their column. When we come to a crossroads, we'll turn right and beat it.'

But Reppa was not in luck. Just as he prepared to pull out, a tank loaded with paratroopers pulled up in front of the house. They rushed the house, weapons at the ready. One of them cried in English, 'Come out!'

Reppa looked at his men, then at the stairs which led to the second floor, filled with wounded. 'We can't make it,' he murmured, 'We can't do a damn thing.'

He crossed slowly to the door, opened it and raising his hands, cried '*Kamerad!*'

Very few Americans offered any resistance at Honsfeld that morning. Here and there a lone soldier tried to fight it out, but with the SS and the paratroopers pouring in from all sides, it was mainly a mad scramble to get out of the town. The tank destroyers, which were supposed to defend the town, were quickly overrun by the paratroopers, and the rear-echelon personnel—cooks, drivers, clerks—scattered wildly in all directions. Guns and vehicles jammed on the exit roads were abandoned. Equipment—gas masks, helmets, overcoats, rifles— was dumped rapidly as the men fled in panic-stricken little groups. Now the cry was '*sauve qui peut!*'

Some four thousand miles away, in New York City, few of those who were reading their Sunday papers at about the time that Jochen Peiper captured Honsfeld read much about the new German offensive in the Belgian Ardennes. In the *New York Times*, the story of the attack appeared on page 19. And even when the more thorough reader finally chanced upon the story, its headline was hardly alarming. 'German Assault On First Army Fierce' was followed by the reassuring sub-head: 'Enemy Pays Heavy Price In Futile Blow To Stem Hodges' Advance.'

Nor was the mood any more alarmist at General Eisenhower's headquarters, which, located as they were at Versailles, were several thousand miles closer to the scene of the action. General

Strong, Eisenhower's Chief Intelligence Officer, had interrupted the vital replacement conference to break the news of the German attack to Bradley and Eisenhower, and during the night his staff had identified some seventeen German divisions in the enemy's order of battle, but in the British General's own words, there was 'no undue concern, certainly no panic and Bradley [whose army was being attacked], in common with many others at Supreme Headquarters, remained convinced that the German attack would quickly peter out for the want of resources'.

Eisenhower was not so sanguine. He reminded his staff officers that he had been promoted just before the disastrous German attack on the American Kasserine Pass positions in North Africa. The result had been a severe setback for the U.S. Army. Now he had been promoted again, to the rank of five-star general, and the Germans had sneaked another counter-attack on him. On the whole he was inclined to accept Bradley's advice and minimise the whole thing, but he had the memory of Kasserine and he decided to send what reinforcements he could to General Middleton, whose VIII Corps had apparently been most badly hit by the new attack. At all events he intended to be on the safe side. The order was given out to alert the two airborne divisions—the 82nd and 101st—both still recovering from their heavy losses in Holland. In spite of the fact that their losses in men and equipment had not yet been fully replaced and many of their men were on leave in London and Paris, they were ordered to proceed to Belgium.

At his hotel headquarters in Spa, the commander of the US 1st Army, General Hodges was equally unperturbed. The news of the offensive had taken a considerable time to reach him and when it did, he presumed it was a diversionary attack to draw him from his drive on the Roer which was being carried out further north by General Gerow's V Corps.

His subordinate, General Gerow, the meticulous infantryman in charge of V Corps who had studied with Eisenhower for a year at the Command and General Staff School before the war, sensed the significance of the attack on the 16th earlier than his chief. He asked Hodges' permission to defend his Corps front as best he could and in any way he saw fit.

Just before dawn on the 17th, he got that permission and started to withdraw the battered 99th Division to a better defensive position on the Elsenborn Ridge some six miles north-west of the scene of battle. At the same time he cancelled the 2nd Division's attack on the Roer and began to feed it and the 1st Infantry Division into the Elsenborn Ridge line at the side of the green 99th. With these two veteran divisions at its side he reckoned that the 99th would be able to hold the line, regardless of what the Germans brought up.

The withdrawal to the Elsenborn Ridge, the northernmost shoulder of the American line facing the enemy penetration—or 'bulge'—was one of the most decisive moves of the whole battle, but at the time no one realised it. It would eventually mean the defeat of *Kampfgruppe* Peiper, but that morning all it meant to him was that the pressure was relieved from his northern flank. Suddenly he was able to proceed almost unopposed.

By dawn Peiper was faced with the tough decision as to whether or not he should expressly disobey the Fuehrer's order to stay on his assigned route. He was already running low on fuel because of the failure of the supply system. Now he had learned from Intelligence that there definitely was an Allied fuel dump at Büllingen[1], but Büllingen was on the route assigned to the 12th SS Panzer Division and he knew that anybody who disobeyed the order to stick on his own road could expect to suffer the death penalty.

Yet Peiper was not just 'anybody'. He had disobeyed orders before and he would do so again; he had little respect for

[1] It is hard to obtain information from the inhabitants of the Ardennes, but more than one source has told me that at certain spots along his route, Peiper or his representatives were handed 'green envelopes' supposedly containing secret information. It is also clear from witnesses' statements that Peiper had turncoat French and Belgian soldiers with him during his advance, who possibly carried out an intelligence mission.

authority, either Party, SS or Army. He needed that fuel if he was to keep rolling to the Meuse and he needed it *now*. Peiper ordered his unit on to Route C. Swiftly he rolled into Büllingen, overcame a small American garrison of engineers, destroyed twelve American liaison planes on the ground, and captured 50,000 gallons of fuel, which he forced fifty American prisoners to pour into his tanks, while he kept glancing nervously to the east, had expecting the 12th SS Panzer to arrive at any moment. He neelf not have worried. The 12th was still held up by remnants of the 99th Infantry at the small village of Losheimergraben on the frontier.

By noon Peiper was back on his assigned route, well west of Büllingen. Behind him at some hour and a half's road distance was the bulk of his force. He, as usual, was well up with the point, riding in the Volkswagen jeep driven by Private Zwigert, with Major Diefenthal, commander of the armoured infantry, at his side. Now he was approaching the major crossroads at the six-house hamlet of Baugnez. Here the road from Büllingen led straight on down a steep hill to the little town of Malmédy some two miles away, while another road turned sharp left towards Ligneuville and from there to the town of St Vith, one of the major rail and road junctions of the Ardennes.

But Peiper was not concerned with St Vith, soon to be one of the major objectives of the whole battle. His task was to continue along the St Vith road for eight kilometres until he reached the hamlet of Ligneuville. There he would turn off and commence the steep climb westwards up a third-class road to the town of Stavelot and the bridge across the River Amblève, the first water barrier he would meet on his way to the Meuse.

While he was thus pondering his situation, the column came to a halt. Zwigart swung the jeep out from behind the tank in front at Peiper's command and sped up the road to see what the trouble was. The leading infantry had caught a 'big fish'. A lone American lieutenant-colonel had been happily driving his jeep along the road at a leisurely pace, unaware that the Germans were so close. Now he stood there in the road, his jeep skidded at an angle, his arms in the air.

Peiper jumped out of his command car and began to question the man in English before the American had time to recover. He wanted to know what might be waiting for him at the Baugnez crossroads.

Hidden round the bend from Peiper at exactly that moment, another American jeep was driving slowly down the steep incline from Baugnez towards the town of Malmédy. It contained a lone military policeman, who had finished directing a convoy of the US 7th Armored Division on its way to defend the threatened junction at St Vith. Now he was on his way back to the billet. He had an hour to kill before the next convoy was expected.

The crossroads was empty. In the houses to the right, the farm folk and their refugee 'guests', who were mostly German from the frontier or the cities of the Rhineland, were sitting down to their meagre meal. In the Café Bodarwé, Madame Bodarwé was standing at the kitchen sink chatting with her neighbour Henri Le Joly. It was just before one o'clock when they heard the noise of vehicles grinding up the incline from Malmédy in low gear. Le Joly looked out of the kitchen window and turned to Madame Bodarwé. '*Ami*,' he said laconically. The women nodded absent-mindedly. Together they watched the American convoy approach the top of the hill. It was Battery B of the 285th Field Artillery Observation Battalion, which was making its way from the Hürtgen Forest to the town of Vielsalm. It was a relatively green outfit, as yet unattached to any corps or division, but it was to achieve greater glory in the manner of its death than it had ever done in its life. Somehow or other, today no one knows how, it had squeezed itself unwittingly between the convoys of the 7th Armored Division and was trying to find its way to the action reported to be taking place on the so-called 'Ghost Front'.

At the crossroads, one of the leading jeeps came to a halt, and a soldier who looked like an officer to Le Joly, followed by two others entered the café. 'Vielsalm?' the leader inquired, and pointed down the road. Madame Bodarwé nodded her agreement.

'*Avez-vous vu les Allemands?*' he asked Le Joly. The farmer pretended not to speak French though he had been speaking Walloon French with Madame Bodarwé just before the Americans had entered. Le Joly was basically German. He and his father had been born in Germany before this territory had been handed over to Belgium at the Treaty of Versailles. He made no pretence of hiding the fact that he hoped Germany would win the war. He contented himself with shaking his head grumpily. The American shrugged and prepared to leave the café

At that moment the first half-track of Peiper's force topped the rise to the east. At once the air was filled with the sound of gunfire. An American truck went up in flames. The convoy skidded to a sudden halt. A jeep careered ahead as its driver bailed out into a ditch. The Americans scattered in all directions, while Le Joly tried to comfort Madame Bodarwé. 'Shall we go into the cellar?' she asked. Le Joly shook his head. 'No, the barn if anywhere. If the house burns down we can't get out of the cellar.'

But they had no time to run for the barn. The shooting was over almost as soon as it had started. Outside the Americans were coming out of the ditches, throwing down their weapons and raising their hands above their heads. Suddenly the kitchen was full of eighteen-year-old German soldiers, their camouflaged coveralls thick with mud and dirt.

At that moment Peiper drove up, shouting to the grenadiers to stop firing. He had just learned from the captive US colonel that there was an *Ami* general quartered in the Hotel du Moulin at Ligneuville. Did they want to warn the general?

As the firing died away the young SS men set about rounding up their prisoners, who came up the road chattering and shouting at each other, as if there was nothing to be feared in this sudden change in their fortunes.

Peiper rapped out a few orders, got back in his jeep, and moved off in the direction of Ligneuville, following the Tiger tanks he had placed in the lead. Behind him most of the point clambered into their vehicles and followed him.

Now the crossroads was deserted again save for the Americans, a handful of young soldiers and two tanks left to guard the prisoners. Full of curiosity, the two Belgians walked out of the dingy café and watched the *Amis*, now grouped together in a field, some fifty metres to the right. A little while later they were joined by a fifteen-year-old refugee boy from the frontier region named Pfeiffer.

The Germans were in an excited, vengeful mood. Back in Büllingen they had taken a hundred prisoners. Some of these had been shut up in a cellar, and three of them, having killed a guard with a pocketknife, had managed to escape. Now the young SS men were thirsting for revenge. Henri Le Joly, happy though he was to see the Germans back again—and he had always thought they would come back—was worried. He knew there was going to be trouble.

General Timberlake, commander of the 49th Anti-Aircraft Brigade, whose job it was to protect the town of Liège some thirty miles to the rear, had just finished lunch in the Hotel du Moulin at Ligneuville. The time was two o'clock.

But if General Timberlake and his staff felt at ease, the population of the hamlet certainly did not. All morning they had been seeing stragglers retreating from the front passing through the village on their way to Vielsalm. Some were armed, some were not; all were a little ashamed and very eager to get to the rear.

Earlier a large convoy of the 7th Armored Division had stopped in the village and heartened the citizens somewhat, but when they came out of Mass it was gone and all that now remained to defend the village were General Timberlake's anti-aircraft gunners and a handful of supply men from the 9th Armored Division, who had arrived with their trucks late the previous night and billeted themselves in the village at the orders of their CO, Captain Seymour Green. When the latter was asked what was going on, he shrugged his shoulders and said all he knew was that he had been ordered to stay in Ligneuville and wait for two other supply trains to arrive.

Time passed slowly. The firing to the east grew louder. Here and there villagers who had no reason to fear the return of the Germans packed a few pathetic possessions in their carpet bags and sneaked out of the village to climb the steep hill behind the hotel which led to Stavelot. But most stayed. Monsieur Hubert Lemaire, the village treasurer, worked in his study. Mlle Locher went into the barn to check her cows. And Herr Rupp, the owner of the village's biggest hotel, who in spite of his German name and the fact that he had been born 69 years previously in that country was an ardent patriot, was not going to flee. All the same he was nervous and kept glancing out of the window of the chalet he occupied next to the hotel. He had a wife and daughter —and the hotel—to think of.

At two o'clock exactly the sound of firing grew much louder. This time it was very close. Through the window Rupp saw a Sherman which had lost a track and was undergoing a hasty repair, firing for all it was worth up the hill towards Baugnez. From behind the hotel a battery of General Timberlake's anti-aircraft guns joined in. The noise shook the chalet and Rupp ducked instinctively.

Now a bulldozer came charging down the hill, rattling at every seam. 'Germans—tanks—lot of them!' the driver cried excitedly to Captain Green who had rushed out of the hotel at the sound of the firing. 'I was shot at by German tanks.'

The Captain reacted at once. 'Get ready to move,' he yelled to his First Sergeant. Then he jumped into his jeep and ordered the driver to take him up the hill in the direction of the Germans. They disappeared up the steep incline in second gear.

At the hotel everything was suddenly panic. General Timberlake's staff did not wait to collect even their personal possessions. Seizing their weapons and helmets, they piled into their vehicles and disappeared in the direction of Vielsalm. A few minutes later General Timberlake appeared, followed by three officers and a woman carrying a child. They, too, drove off hurriedly. Now the hotel was empty, the used plates still on the table in the big dark dining-room, maps of the front with the symbols indicating the location of Timberlake's units on the wall, his best uniform still hanging in the closet in his bedroom. The Hôtel du Moulin waited for its new occupants.

2

Captain Green clutched his carbine a little tighter and ordered the driver to stop. The man didn't like the assignment and Green knew it. Now he would go on alone. Gratefully the driver pulled up at the top of the incline before the road followed a sharp curve cut between two embankments. 'I'm going ahead to do some snooping. If anything happens, go back.' Green ordered.

Slowly he edged his way round the bend. Less than fifty yards away there was a scout car. On its camouflaged side there was a great black cross. Behind it was a long line of half-tracks filled with heavily-armed infantrymen. Green stood rooted to the spot, all the energy drained out of his body. Even when the Germans spotted him, he did not move. Finally he dropped his carbine and raised his hands in surrender. An officer with a pistol in his hand waved him to the side of the road.

Now the column started to move again. Several of the men in the half-tracks made threatening gestures with their machine pistols as they clattered past and then laughed when they saw the look of alarm in the young American captain's face.

The tanks rumbled swiftly down the steep incline, firing as they went. A German half-track was hit and slewed to a halt, bursting into flames a moment later. Frantically the grenadiers baled out, their clothes blazing. A Tiger stopped and took deliberate aim at the Sherman. Desperately the American gunner pumped round after round at the advancing Germans. Another half-track was hit. Expertly the grenadiers swung themselves over the metal sides and ran for cover. It too went up in flames. The Tiger had now got the Sherman's range. His first shot missed; he fired again and this time his aim was true. There was a loud echoing sound of metal striking metal. The Sherman rocked from side to side and stopped firing. The German column raced on, past the Hotel du Moulin, shooting up the last of Green's trucks as they sped up the hill and out of the range of the slower tanks.

The twenty-two American prisoners, some of them wounded, were hustled roughly into the hotel lounge. The Germans spread through the house, noisy and triumphant, machine pistols held at the ready, laughing and shouting to one another at the sight of the American officers' uniforms still hanging in the closets.

Meanwhile Sergeant Paul Ochmann of Peiper's headquarters company, followed by two other men, was striding up the littered village street trying to find a place for eight American prisoners who walked in front of him, their faces sunk in defeat, their hands above their heads. They were Sergeant Abraham Lincoln and seven other men of the 843rd Tank Division, whom Ochmann had forced out of the hotel at the point of his machine pistol. But none of the little houses seemed to suit the Sergeant. Suddenly he stopped the procession in front of the village bakery slightly up the slope towards Baugnez. The Americans stopped and stared at their captors. Behind them on the heights, the wrecked German vehicles still smoked heavily. Now the firing had died away save for the crack of cannon somewhere to the rear of the village. Hidden among her cows in the barn, Mlle Locher peeped through a crack in the weathered boards and stared out curiously. Suddenly her eyes grew round with fear and her mouth dropped open. The burly German sergeant had raised his pistol and aimed it at the first prisoner. There was a sharp crack and the man sank to the ground. The next man's hands flew up to his face, as if naked flesh would protect him from the hard metal. The pistol cracked again and again.

Within a matter of seconds it was all over. Privates Carter, Sulivan, Pitts, Penney, Tech 4 and Tech 5 Casper Johnson and John Borcina and Staff-Sergeant Joseph Collins joined Sergeant Lincoln on the cold cobbles of the village street.

Peter Rupp, who had watched the whole scene, forgot his wife, his daughter, the hotel, the product of thirty years of hard work. He forgot everything. Leaving his observation post at the window, he cried at Ochmann, as the latter re-entered the hotel. '*Murderer*, I saw you put the pistol in their mouths!'

The German sergeant, known among his comrades as a quiet reserved man, did not even bother to protest. According to Mr Rupp's statement after the war, the sergeant punched him in the jaw and he staggered back, spitting out blood and teeth.

It was perhaps a quarter of an hour later that Hubert Lemaire crept out of the cellar where he had sheltered during the firing. Now he stared down at the eight corpses stretched out in the gutter. Suddenly a German tank rumbled down the hill and stopped by the bodies. 'What happened here?' the tank commander called to Hubert, who spoke fluent German. Before he could reply, a member of the tank crew said: 'It's obvious, isn't it, sir?' The tank commander nodded. 'Yes, you're right.' Speaking to Lemaire, he said, 'You! Get these bodies buried at once!'

Lemaire nodded and the tank commander, his eyes still fixed on the stiff bodies stretched out in the gutter, gave the order to proceed.[1]

For a short while Peiper rested in the hotel. It had been an eventful day so far. His success at Büllingen, where the Americans had panicked at the sight of his vehicles and fled down the street in disorder, had encouraged him to believe that the operation might be a success after all, if this was all the opposition the *Amis* could put against him. But now he was

[1] Lemaire never got a chance to bury the bodies. A little later a German tank commander ordered him to get on his tank. Reluctantly M. Lemaire obeyed and after an hour's ride on the Tiger he managed to escape and make his way home.

beginning to suffer losses and no supplies or reinforcements, least of all the follow-up infantry, were getting through to him. Only an hour before, he had lost one of his best commanders; Arndt Fischer had struggled out of his burning Panther, his body a living torch. The sight had so angered Peiper that he had seized a *Panzerfaust*[1] himself and gone tank-hunting, but the lone Sherman had been knocked out before he had got within range. Fischer lived but Peiper couldn't afford to go on losing good men. His leading troops would soon be crossing the Amblève and he must be there to see that everything went according to plan. He got to his feet and left the hotel.

Frau Balbina Rupp, Peter's wife, was a pious, hard-working Swiss woman. Years ago when she had first taken over the hotel, she had found twenty pfennigs in the cash register and sixty-four thousand marks in debts in the safe. Undaunted, she had built the hotel up to three-star category and gained for it the reputation of having the finest wine cellar in the whole of Belgium. Madame Rupp was a woman who was persistent, not easily frightened and hard to put down. But on this grim December day, with eight dead bodies sprawled outside her hotel and her husband in danger of the same fate, she was afraid. She did not show it. Hurrying into the hotel just after Peiper left, she pushed her husband through the open door into the cellar and closed it quickly behind him. She turned to find herself facing an officer with an inquiring look on his face. Balbina Rupp reacted quickly, though when it was all over she felt she had to hurry to her priest and confess the lie she had told. 'My husband is not altogether there,' she touched her forehead significantly. 'We never wanted to tell anyone for the sake of the hotel. You mustn't take him seriously.'

The officer grinned, touched his cap and went his way. Peter was safe for the time being. But Balbina Rupp wasn't finished yet. There was the question of the prisoners. She wouldn't rest easily until she got some assurance about their safety. She would

[1] German bazooka.

talk to the German commander. It was surprisingly easy. In a matter of minutes she was speaking to the officer-in-charge.[1] The officer, champagne glass in hand, listened to her understandingly and without interruption while she explained that she was from the Swiss Red Cross, another lie that she had to confess to her priest later, and that she had 'orders to look after all prisoners and see that they get food'.

The German nodded. 'But you must look after our wounded too,' he admonished her. She agreed and, pleased with her success, hurried out to find some food for the Americans.

In the meantime Peter Rupp had recovered his nerve. He called his daughter; 'Mary,' he whispered to her, 'give the guard a good cognac so that I can get in and talk to the prisoners.' His daughter did as she was told and Rupp slipped into the prisoners' room, with a bottle of brandy held in each hand. Captain Green eyed him suspiciously. 'Wait a moment,' 'are you Belgian or German?'

'Belgian,' Rupp answered.

When the Americans had taken a drink of the cognac, passing the bottle from mouth to mouth, Rupp told Green of his fears for their safety after what happened outside. He would do his utmost, he promised them, to ensure that there would be no further shootings. Then he left and took up his position in the lobby, armed with the bottles of wine and cognac that Mary had brought up from the cellar. For the rest of the evening he handed a bottle to every German soldier in sight.

The soldiers needed no urging to accept the unexpected gifts. Without bothering about glasses, they upended the brown bottles time and time again.

The atmosphere in the darkening lobby grew cordial, then jovial. The hard-faced SS troopers relaxed, became friendly,

---

[1] After the war, the Rupps told Allied interrogators that the officer was Sepp Dietrich, who took over the hotel with his staff that afternoon. But she was undoubtedly mistaken. Sepp Dietrich was still back in Germany. Indeed how could he have made his way through the bottleneck at Büllingen under the conditions pertaining that afternoon even if he had wished to? But both Eisenhower in *The Bitter Woods* and Toland in *Battle* accept the Dietrich 'legend'.

even a little maudlin. The tension disappeared. Here and there tired and slightly drunken men began to slide down the walls, against which they had supported themselves, and fell asleep on the floor where they lay.

Rupp and his wife knew that they had averted a potential tragedy. The remaining American soldiers had been a burden to the Germans, just as the eight Ochmann had shot had been too troublesome for him so that killing them had been the easiest way out. A few hours before it had been on the cards that the SS would have shot them too. Now the killing mood had passed; the young Germans whom Peiper had left behind were too tired to care, too tired—and too drunk. A heavy silence descended on the Hôtel du Moulin. Outside, the eight who had been so savagely slaughtered a few hours before began to stiffen in the ice-cold air.

3

But while the courageous efforts of Monsieur and Madame Rupp had averted a further atrocity at the Hôtel du Moulin, there was no brave Belgian at the lonely Baugnez crossroads to prevent the tragedy which was soon to take place there.

At about the same time that Captain Seymour Green found himself facing Peiper's advance guard, the bulk of *Kampfgruppe* Peiper started to pull round the Baugnez corner, coming from the direction of Büllingen, watched by the three curious civilians at the Café Bodarwé and the American prisoners huddled together in the field some fifty metres away. For a while the Germans concentrated on getting their monstrous sixty-ton Tigers around the tight bend in the direction of Ligneuville. One of them standing on the turret of a Panther called out cheerily to the American prisoners, 'It's a long way to Tipperary, boys!'[1]

[1] Later on it was established that this was Peiper himself. In years to come he was to regret it, since the remark helped to identify him as one of the 'Malmédy killers' after the war.

Not one of the glum prisoners-of-war answered him. He shrugged his shoulders and kicking his driver on the shoulder, signalled him to drive the tank on. Then for some reason a self-propelled gun armed with a huge 88 mm cannon stopped

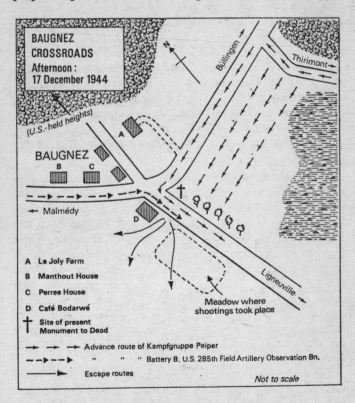

opposite the prisoners and swung its terrifying weapon in their direction. Young Second Lieutenant Virgil Lary, standing in the front row of the Americans, swallowed hard as the hand-cranked gun bore down on them. It seemed to be pointed directly at him. Were the Krauts going to open fire?

He never got an answer to his unspoken question. The SP was blocking the road to Ligneuville and an officer angrily ordered it to get out of the way. With a grinding of gears and a clank of metal tracks, it turned and rattled off southwards. An embarrassed American lieutenant-colonel then appeared, driving his own jeep, under the guard of two grinning teenage SS men. There were about 150 men in the field now, including a fair number of Medical Corps men still wearing their Red Cross brassards on their arms.

Another few minutes passed. Vehicle after vehicle swung south, throwing up showers of mud as they rounded the corner. Then for no apparent reason two armoured vehicles came to a halt, directly facing the prisoners. In the first vehicle, belonging to the 7th Tank Company and commanded by Sergeant Hans Siptrott, a young Rumanian soldier took out his pistol and looked towards the prisoners.

He was Private First Class Georg Fleps, one of the foreign soldiers drafted into the SS in their thousands in 1942 and 1943 to make up for the losses suffered in Russia. Fleps' forefathers had left their Swabian homeland in the Middle Ages and emigrated to the Seven Mountains area of Rumania, where they had founded prosperous little farming communities, cut off from their less industrous neighbours by their German dialect and their German industry. When Rumania joined the Nazi cause, Himmler, the head of the SS, had seen the country as a source of recruits. Overnight these German citizens of Rumania became *Volksdeutsche* (Ethnic Germans) and eligible for entry even to the most élite SS formation of all—the *Leibstandarte*.

The native-born Germans in the Division called them 'booty Germans' behind their backs but realised that the *Leibstandarte* would not be able to function without them. So they were accepted, Rumanians, Hungarians, Alsatians, Belgians, even a few 'racially inferior' Frenchmen, who in an attempt to bolster up their lack of German birth were often more fanatical and ruthless than their native-born comrades. Georg Fleps, the

21-year-old private from the Seven Mountains, was such a 'booty German'.

Raising his pistol he took careful aim. Then he fired. Once. Twice. His first shot could not miss. Lary's driver, standing in the front row of the prisoners, groaned out loud, clutched his chest and fell. For what seemed an eternity the prisoners stared aghast at the man on the ground, the blood pouring from a chest wound, as if they simply could not believe that this could happen to American soldiers. At the door of the café Henri Le Joly watched the scene with horror.

Then the machine-guns started to chatter. The massacre had begun.

A sudden atavistic fury seemed to overcome the Germans. Everywhere the tankers and combat engineers of the *Kampfgruppe* began to fire into the massed ranks of the Americans. '*Stand fast!*' an officer cried desperately, trying to avoid a mass stampede and himself fell dead a moment later.

The prisoners started to fall in groups, as other machine guns joined in the slaughter. They were completely defenceless. Some tried to make a break for it, but were mown down before they'd gone half-a-dozen yards. A few raised their hands and covered their eyes, as if by blotting out the whole scene they would make it go away. Wounded, dead and dying were everywhere in the bloody grass and still the machine-guns went on.

Some of the Americans had realised that this was a massacre almost as soon as the machine-guns opened up. Lary, who had been wounded in the first salvo, fell to the ground and feigned death. He held his breath fearfully and waited for the firing to stop. So did Homer D. Ford, a military policeman; Ken Ahrens was another. As was Samuel Dobyns, a medic, who had gone through Normandy and been recommended for rescuing German wounded under fire. Perhaps twenty in all were now lying under the bloody shambles waiting for the murderous fire to end.

Finally it stopped. First the machine-guns, then the rifles, petering away to individual pistol shots. Then there was silence.

Those who were still alive waited tensely, their faces wet with the sweat of fear.

They did not have to wait long. Lary heard a pistol shot close by and the sound of boots wading through the dead. He closed his eyes and held his breath as the sound of the boots came closer and closer. Once it stopped and Lary thought he had been spotted. Then the sound continued, was parallel with him, and passed on.

Lary squinted out of the corner of his eye. Another German was coming towards him. He was kicking each body in a systematic manner, as if he did this sort of thing every day, aiming his heavy steel-tipped boot viciously at the lying men's faces. When here and there, a supposedly 'dead' man flinched, he fired a bullet into the dormant figure. Now others were taking up this macabre sport, laughing idiotically as they did so. 'Maniacal', was Lary's description of the sound many years later.[1]

But Samuel Dobyns was not prepared to die like a dumb animal. Summoning all his strength, he got up and begun to run. There was a cry of rage. A machine-gun opened up. The first burst caught him only twenty yards from the scene of the slaughter. Four slugs entered his body, eight others ripped his clothes to tatters. Heavily he hit the ground, bleeding profusely. Three SS came towards him. Then abruptly they turned back. Perhaps they thought he was already dead. Dobyns did not know, nor did he care. He felt he was dying anyway.

There weren't many left alive now. A few wounded men had managed to crawl across the road to the houses of the local farmers. But the SS did not allow them to enter. Paul Pfeiffer, the fifteen-year-old boy who had taken refuge in the Poree house saw how those who could still crawl were allowed to enter a barn. The rest were left on the road.

In the Manthont house, where by a cruel twist of fate one son

[1] In Russia the SS had been used to giving their own seriously wounded the *coup de grâce* by means of a bullet through the neck when no medical aid was available, as was the case at the Baugnez crossroads.

was in the SS himself and the other in a German concentration camp, villagers saw how the tanks coming from Büllingen ran over the bodies sprawled in the road. Whether the Americans were dead or not, they couldn't see. Horrified, they looked away as another tank rumbled round the corner and crushed the inert figures.

The *Blutrausch*[1] was almost over. Now there were only a few German vehicles left at the cross-roads. The groans ceased. The bloodied grass and churned mud around the café were littered with over a hundred and fifty men, of whom eighty-four were dead, the rest badly wounded.

The last German left the field shouting for his comrades to wait for him, and silence fell on the scene of the massacre.

The Café Bodarwé was in flames and Madame Bodarwé had disappeared, never to be seen again.[2] Henri Le Joly had flown too. He had enough sense to realise that eye-witnesses of what had happened that afternoon were not going to live long. While the firing was still going on he had slunk away across the road and up the lane to his own farm.

Now, perhaps half an hour after the massacre, he too was in trouble. A German tank had stopped on the road from Büllingen opposite the little lane that led to the farm. Hesitantly Le Joly walked up to it. Suddenly one of the two eighteen-year-old boys on the turret pulled out a pistol and pointed it at him. He thought of what Fleps had done at the corner. '*Ich bin doch deutsch!*' he protested.

The young soldier did not seem to hear. He fired at twenty metres range and missed. Le Joly turned and pelted panic-stricken back to his house and clattered down the stone steps

[1] An almost untranslatable German phrase, meaning roughly 'Intoxication of the blood'.

[2] Louis Bodarwé, her son, told the author that when he returned to his ruined home immediately after the war and set about digging into the rubble, he found a severed leg, which was later identified as that of a woman. Some time later the village of Aue, which lies on the German side of the border, reported finding a woman minus a leg. Thinking that the body might be that of his mother, he went to the village but by that time the woman had been buried and the local authorities refused to allow him to have it exhumed.

into the cellar. In it he found an elderly German refugee, a former First World War soldier who came from Cologne, and an eighteen-year-old Belgian youth whom he did not know.

There was no time for introductions. As he flung the door closed behind him, there was a great roar, followed by a tremendous blast. The cellar rocked. Dust and pieces of plaster poured down on the three men. A shell from the tank had destroyed the kitchen above.

'Why are they shooting at us!' the old man cried. 'We're German.' He turned to Le Joly. 'Tell them we are German and they are still in Germany.'

Obediently Henri did as he was told. He clambered up the stairs and waded through the rubble of his shattered kitchen. A sergeant was standing on the turret of the tank now, staring down the path. He crooked a finger at Henri, gesturing him to come forward. Henri shook his head and crooked his finger in turn at the NCO. Followed by the two boys, the NCO advanced cautiously down the muddy farm path. 'Why are you shooting at me?' Henri demanded angrily as the man came close. 'We're as German as you. My father fought in the Great War and my grandfather in the War of '70.' Behind him now was the man from Cologne who had come up the stairs. He said, 'That's right, I am German. I fought in the Great War.' He held out his paybook with the names of the battles in which he had fought.

The SS *Unteroffizier* cast a quick glance at it and then handed it back. 'We saw someone running across the fields to the house. We thought he was an *Ami* or a partisan.'

Henri realised they were talking about the strange boy in the cellar. He did not react, but changed the subject quickly. Seeing the smoke coming from the café, he said, 'Can't you stop the fire?'

The NCO shook his head. 'No time for that. We've got a war to fight.'

Now the two young soldiers were beginning to make threatening gestures. One of them shouted, 'I'll take you into the field and shoot you!' 'But I'm as German as you—' Le Joly began.

The young soldier cut him short. 'You're all spies and traitors at the border,' he yelled.

Hastily the NCO pushed himself between the two excited youths and the Belgian. 'Get back to your cellar,' he hissed. 'I can't restrain them much longer.'

Le Joly fled.

Ken Ahrens was wounded twice in the back, but he was still alive. The long motionless wait for the last of the Germans to go away had left him frozen from head to foot. But still he could feel the pain of the two wounds in his back.

Lary was also still alive. A bullet had severed his toes and the pain was crippling, but at least he was alive. Here and there whispered voices were raised. 'Have they gone? What shall we do? Is it safe? Shall we run for it? What about the badly wounded? Too bad. It's every man for himself. NOW! LET'S GO!'

About fifteen or twenty men levered themselves up. There seemed to be no Germans about. They began to run. Suddenly rifles started firing. The group scattered wildly. Some headed for a house but a machine-gun burst caught them half-way.

Lary clambered over a fence and ran along a dirt road until he came to a tumbledown shed. Opening the door he peered into the gloom searching for a hiding place. In the corner was a pile of sticks. Hurriedly he buried himself under them and waited.

Ahrens headed for a wood about two hundred yards away. His heart was thumping and his breath coming in gulps but he made it. For a moment, he paused steadying himself weakly against a tree. He knew he could't stay there long. The Germans were sure to find him. Summoning up the last of his strength, he staggered through the wet underbrush, dribbling blood behind him, heading for a town whose name would soon signify to the western world one thing only—massacre. The town was called Malmédy.

4

All day long tanks and trucks had been rumbling, bumper to bumper, through the cobbled streets of the medieval town of Stavelot, their decks strewn with jerricans, spare tracks, weapons, bedrolls and sleeping men. This was the US 7th Armored Division, heading for the little Belgian town of St Vith.

Occasionally the column halted to allow one of the Shermans to negotiate a sharp corner, and crowds of anxious citizens besieged the soldiers with questions, only to be told, 'Don't worry, we're just changing positions.'

Towards midday they heard on both the BBC and on Brussels Radio that there had been a breakthrough at Echternach in Luxemburg, which the American forces were containing without any great difficulty. But their relief soon evaporated when American combat engineers began to set up a machine-gun position opposite the narrow stone bridge across the River Amblève.

Their anxiety increased when a handful of adventurous youths, who had climbed the heights to the east of the town overlooking the hill road from Ligneuville, ran back around 3.30 and reported that they had seen thick pillars of black smoke rising from the little village of Waimes near Ligneuville. Half an hour later the rumour spread through the town that the authorities were evacuating Malmédy.

In September when the Germans had retreated before the advancing Americans, the beaten Boche had called out to the jeering townsfolk, 'We'll be back in two months, you wait and see!' Now it seemed they were going to make good their threat.

Crouched in their stuffy kitchens, the former Resistance workers debated all afternoon what they should do. They had helped to defeat the Germans in September, sneaking through the German lines to give the advancing Americans information about the enemy positions in the town. Now the returning Germans would know their names; the border area was full of spies. Should they flee while they still had time? Henri

Daisoment, who had helped the Americans in September, and who was soon to be shot together with his wife and two girls, said categorically: 'If I am to die, I'll die here. I don't want to go through May, 1940 again.'

At 4.30, as dusk began to fall, the first refugees from Ligneu-ville started to arrive in the town. At five o'clock they were followed by refugees from Malmédy. The rumour was true. They were evacuating Malmédy. At six, everyone knew that the Germans were coming for the third time this century, and the Burgomaster ordered the bellringers to sound the curfew. As the bells boomed out their first warning notes, the frightened citizens hurried through the dark to their homes. Doors were barred, windows were shuttered. Food and water were taken down into the deep medieval cellars, cut into the rock of the steep cliff which rose on the west bank of the river. Now in the flickering light of the candles, which threw gigantic shadows on the dripping walls, the frightened citizens of Stavelot waited, while outside the tanks of the 7th Armored continued to rattle through the empty streets.

Stavelot lies in the valley of the Amblève River, surrounded by high, sparsely-wooded cliffs. Most of the town, at that time, was built on the northern bank of the river, reaching up to the top of the slope. On the south side was a single row of houses. Like most of the many streams and rivers in this part of the Ardennes, the Amblève presented no great obstacle to infantry, except for the icy coldness of its water in wintertime. But the deeply-cut valley and the awkwardness of the approach, down a steep road with a sharp bend, made the Amblève a tougher-than-average tank-barrier, especially for the 60-ton monsters which made up part of Peiper's force. But in spite of the difficulty of the terrain, Stavelot with its five thousand inhabitants and its vital bridge, which Peiper must have if he wanted to take the direct route to the Meuse, was open for the asking as night fell on the 17th December. At that moment there was exactly one squad of the 291st Combat Engineer Battalion defending the town; Stavelot could be Peiper's by nightfall

By dusk he had caught up with his advance guard and as usual went straight to the point, which at that moment was taking the corner that turned round a huge rock and then on to the bridge itself.

From where his vehicle stopped while the first tank took the difficult bend, it seemed to Peiper that Stavelot was a small-scale fortress, with its red-brick eighteenth-century houses and warehouses rising up from the river like a castle wall. But his men did not hesitate. Three tanks had now rounded the corner and were rumbling towards the bridge itself. A few moments more and they were over. Then suddenly there was a muffled roar, a sheet of violet flame shot from under the first tank. It rocked from side to side and came to an abrupt halt. It had gone over the first of a hastily-laid daisy chain of anti-tank mines spread by the engineers across the road. As if the explosion of the mine were a signal, a thin crackle of sniper fire came from the first row of houses on the north side of the Amblève. A moment later a slow ·50 calibre American machine-gun joined in, sending a stream of white and green tracer bullets through the darkness.

Peiper frowned and rubbed his chin. It seemed there were plenty of Americans in Stavelot. Through his night glasses he could see the trucks of the 7th Armored passing through the main square on their way to St Vith. Swiftly he made a decision. Ordering Lieutenant Sternebeck to pull back from the bridge, he dispatched a tank company to check out the road which wound south of the River Amblève to the bridge at Trois Ponts. If he could take that one he would not need the bridge at Stavelot.

The tanks rumbled off and Peiper looked round at his men. Most of them were asleep; they had not slept for nearly three days and many of them had not eaten much in that period either. Suddenly Peiper realised that he too was tired. Just like his men, he wanted nothing but sleep. It was then that he made a decision which was fatal to his whole operation. He decided to wait for the information about the road to Trois Ponts and attack Stavelot at first light the next morning. Drained of energy, he gave the command to his officers to bed down for the night.

Back at Malmédy Lieutenant-Colonel Peregrin, CO of the engineer battalion stationed in the town, had been alarmed by the noise of firing at the Baugnez crossroads. He knew that the 285th Field Artillery Observation Battery had gone that way shortly before and putting two and two together, he figured that the outfit had run into trouble. Collecting one of his NCOs, Sergeant Bill Crickenberger, who was armed with a sub-machine-gun, the two men drove up to the high ground over-looking the crossroads. There they parked the jeep and began to make their way cautiously on foot to a wooded area not far from the crossroads.

Suddenly three Americans broke out of the bushes to their front. Crickenberger raised his sub-machine-gun automatically. 'Stop!' Peregrin cried. 'They're our boys!'

Crickenberger's mouth dropped open in bewilderment. He had never seen GIs like that before. They were ragged and tattered, their rags covered in blood, and, as Colonel Peregrin remembered later, 'screaming incoherently ... something about a massacre'. They were Virgil Lary, Homer Ford and another man. The shocked Colonel and his NCO hurried towards the three survivors, who were utterly broken by what had happened to them that afternoon, and tried to comfort them as they led them to the jeep. Then they sped back to the Battalion Aid Station in Malmédy.

Just as they arrived, two newspapermen, Hal Boyle and Jack Belden of *Time Magazine* drove up in their jeep from First Army Headquarters at Spa. That morning the two journalists had risen late, having been to a party the night before. While the rest of the correspondents had already gone 'up the front', taking round-about roads to reach the scene of the newly-reported German breakthrough, Boyle and Beldon had taken a leisurely breakfast and set off on their own. Boyle had been through the Battle of the Kasserine Pass in North Africa and reckoned he knew the speed of the German panzer divisions. Although the staff officers at HQ had told him that the Germans couldn't get so far so quickly, he assured his companion that the Baugnez crossroads was the likeliest spot to see some action and thither they had gone.

Now, hardened as they were, they were silent and shocked as the three bloody survivors told their stories, 'half-frozen, dazed, weeping with anger,' as Boyle wrote later. While the medics hurried to attend to them and someone ran out to fetch hot coffee, young Lieutenant Lary shook the bullet out of his boot and with it the bloody remains of his toes. 'We didn't have a chance,' he sobbed, 'We didn't have a chance . . . '

It was the story of the war for the two newspapermen. Quickly they took down what they could from the three survivors and drove at top speed back to Spa to file their stories. By six o'clock that evening it had been passed to the Inspector-General of the 1st Army. Incensed by the story of the massacre, he ordered that maximum publicity should be given to it. The news rose the ladder of command to the 1st Army's Chief-of-Staff, Major-General William Kean, who noted in his diary that evening. 'There is absolutely no question as to its proof—immediate publicity is being given to the story. General Quesada[1] has told every one of his pilots about it during their briefing.'

The soldiers' newspaper *Stars and Stripes* promised to run it on their front page in their next day's issue. *Soldatensender Calais*, the fake 'German' station, actually run by German refugees and former prisoners-of-war under the command of Sefton Delmer, promised to broadcast the news of the atrocity back to Germany. Everywhere the American command began to organise a great propaganda effort to highlight the viciousness of the German counter-attack, 'the European Pearl Harbour', as it was soon to be called, and bolster the flagging morale of the American troops.

By late evening the rumour that the SS were shooting American prisoners-of-war had reached the front line divisions. Everywhere combat commanders told their men. 'We're not

---

Commander of the 9th TAC Air Force.

taking any Krauts prisoner this time, fellers. 'Specially if they're SS.'

Here and there written orders were actually issued to this effect, such as that of the 328th Infantry Regiment, giving instructions for an attack to be launched the following day: '*No SS troops or paratroopers will be taken prisoner, but will be shot on sight . . .* '

And in a tall echoing office tucked away in the great SHAEF complex at Versailles clerks began the job of collecting names, dates, places, pertaining to the massacre of an unknown number of American soldiers by an unknown German SS formation.

On that December evening they started to fashion the noose intended to hang Jochen Peiper, an attempt which was to shake the whole foundation of American military justice and involve the person of the Supreme Commander himself when he later held the office of President of the United States.

Far away on the lonely crossroads at Baugnez the snow had begun to fall and soon it covered the dead soldiers with a mantle of white. By midnight their contorted bodies were no longer to be seen.

Day Three:

MONDAY, 18 DECEMBER, 1944

'General, if you dont want to be captured, you'd better get out of town! The Germans are only a mile away.'

Colonel Dickson to General Hodges,
Commander, US 1st Army.

Colonel 'Monk' Dickson fell exhausted into his bed at 1 am on the eighteenth. He had only enjoyed one day in Paris after that prophetic intelligence summary of 15 December. On the evening of the following day when, even to his own surprise, his prophecy had come true, he had been told indirectly that he should go at once to see his opposite number on General Bradley's staff, Brigadier-General Edwin Sibert, at the Hotel Alpha in Luxemburg. His informant had told him little but the 'Monk' realised the seriousness of the situation.

By dawn he was on his way. Arriving at the sleazy hotel opposite the city's main railway station, he was ushered immediately into Sibert's office and shown the operations map. He saw at once how bad the situation was.

His next stop was General Middleton's HQ at Bastogne. There the situation was even worse. It was obvious that Middleton's VIII Corps had been very badly hit indeed and the mood of both officers and men he saw around him convinced him that they were suffering from an acute attack of nerves. Having conferred with Middleton he set off once more just after dark, heading up the main road towards Liège. There were few US troops about and those he met at cross-roads and check-points were nervous and tense, their fingers itchy on the triggers.

Dickson settled back and tried to sleep, but his racing brain would not allow him to. Middleton had lost the 106th Division, with two of its regiments surrounded in the Eifel hills. The 14th Cavalry did not exist any more. The key town of St Vith was already under attack and it could not be long before Bastogne itself would suffer the same fate. Dickson bit his bottom lip thoughtfully. He would have a lot to tell Hodges when he got to Spa.

They went past Werbomont which, unknown to Dickson, was to be Peiper's objective on the morrow once he had taken Stavelot and Trois Ponts. Soon they were approaching the crossroads town of Aywaille where they would turn off for Spa. Suddenly a patrol came out of the shadows and ordered the car to slow down. They were men of the T Force, a special reconnaissance outfit of three-hundred picked men whose job it was to be the eyes and ears of the 12th Army Group.

The T Force commander was Colonel Tommy Tompkins, an old friend of Dickson's. He asked him what he was up to. Tompkins told him that T Force had been given the task of protecting Spa from a Nazi armoured column reported to be in Malmédy or Stavelot. 'If I were you, Monk,' he said, 'I'd go all the way north, then turn back to Spa by way of Theux. It's longer but it's certainly safer.'

Dickson knew that his friend was not one to overestimate a danger. He thanked him and set off on the longer route, thinking, 'If 12th Army Group is using its T Force for this kind of a job, then they're really scraping the barrel.'

Finally he reached Spa. The once-fashionable watering town was now filled with a mass of supply trucks evacuating the huge supply dumps. Although it was already very late the pavements were crowded with soldiers and civilians feverishly loading trucks and staff cars. Forcing its way through the throng, Dickson's driver deposited him in front of Hodges' hotel where nearly a quarter of a century before, Kaiser William the Second had signed his abdication and ended the Second Reich. Hastily he made his way to General Hodges and told his superior everything he had heard and seen that day; and although he knew he was regarded as a confirmed pessimist at headquarters, he felt that this time his gloomy prognosis was justified. He finished his report, gave Hodges a moment to think and then made his final recommendation. 'General, I think you ought to move this C.P. out of this place tomorrow.' Then he went to bed.

General Hodges, Commander of the 1st US Army in World War II, was, and has remained, something of an enigma. He was a competent but shy man who was almost ordered at times to try to improve his public image. For instance, Commander Butcher, Eisenhower's Public Relations Chief, officially told his PR men that they should soft-pedal General Patton's exploits and try to get some publicity for the almost unknown Hodges, but inevitably Patton always outshone the retiring commander of the First Army.

Perhaps the key to Hodges' personality was a frustrated past, in which Patton played a leading role. In early '44 he had commanded the Third Army in England, then Patton had supplanted him. Later in France, Patton again seemed to dominate, for (as it seemed to Hodges who had never held a field command before), Bradley seemed to prefer his own former boss, the dramatic, colourful Patton. Although his own army, the First, had taken more than its fair share of the fighting in the summer and autumn of 1944, with their casualties far outnumbering those of Patton's Third, it was always the latter's exploits which hit the headlines, not his own. As a result Hodges seemed to retire even more into his shell, become even more cautious, more of the infantryman he had once been, with the latter's traditionally wary approach to battle, in contrast to Patton's dashing cavalryman's approach, characterised by his favourite motto: '*L'audace, l'audace, toujour l'audace!*'

Now Hodges realised that he had been too careful the previous day. Throughout the sixteenth he had done nothing. On the next day he had twice refused the requests of General Gerow of V Corps to discontinue his attack against the Roer dams and to withdraw in good time to the Elsenborn ridge. The Germans had knocked two distinct gaps in his line, both in the area of the VIII Corps. The northern gap was between the flank of the 2nd and 99th Divisions and the two regiments of the 106th Division cut off in the Eifel hills. The second was some ten to twelve miles in width in the 28th Division's sector to the south. But it was the first gap that worried him; *how much of the armoured force which had attacked Büllingen on the morning of the 17th had got through, and what was the aim of this unit, Spa or Malmédy?*

Now it was clear that the Germans had caught Hodges' troops completely by surprise and that his units were entirely ignorant about the enemy's intentions and objectives. Even the powerful 9th Air Force attached to his command could not help him. The weather had been bad for two days. Thus, it seemed to him, he was like a boxer trying to slug it out with an opponent who could see exactly what he was doing, while he himself was blindfolded.

General Hodges went through his dispositions once more. That morning he had alerted the 30th Infantry Division, which had been out of the line resting in the Aachen area. Since dusk it had been on the road, with the 117th Regiment, commanded by Colonel Walter Johnson, in the lead and heading for the vital Stavelot–Malmédy area. There its 1st battalion was scheduled to hold Stavelot, its 2nd to defend the ridges between Stavelot and Malmédy, with its 3rd defending the town of Malmédy itself.

The 82nd Airborne Division, commanded by 37-year-old General Gavin was also on the road hurrying from its base in France. Underequipped and understrength as a result of severe fighting in Holland of the previous month, the Division was not at its best, but it was still full of fight. Its destination was the area around the town of Werbomont to the south of Spa.

Both divisions were highly competent formations, as Hodges knew, but the question that plagued him was whether they would arrive in time? If they didn't, what would happen to the area to the north of the River Amblève, which was packed with vital First Army installations?

Both Stavelot and Malmédy contained important army dumps, but more significantly the two bridges at the towns could give the unidentified German armoured force, which had broken through at Büllingen, access to the largest fuel dump on the Continent with 2,500,000 gallons of fuel tightly packed into the fir forests between his own headquarters at Spa and the River Amblève. If the Germans captured the dump, their armoured forces, which as Hodges knew from past experience were always chronically short of fuel, would have enough gas to take them to the Meuse!

By the early hours of 18 December, Eisenhower was scraping the bottom of the barrel to bolster the defense of the Amblève River line. He was already beginning to strip the 9th Army's Front, from which the 30th Division and later the 9th were coming. He had thrown in his last reserves on the Continent, the two Airborne Divisions, the 82nd and 101st, to the delight of the Germans who intercepted the radio signal passing on the order and realised that the Americans were in a worse situation than they had suspected.

But all these formations were coming into the line piecemeal and under no overall control. Consequently Eisenhower sent an urgent message to General Matthew Ridgway, Commanding General of the US XVIII Airborne Corps, at the CP of the 17th Airborne Division, in Wiltshire, England.

Ridgway was soon briefed. The Germans were smashing through the Ardennes. Eisenhower had released his two airborne divisions and placed them at First Army's disposal. Both were now on their way to the front.

Ridgway realised the urgency of the situation. His two finest divisions were in France, but most of the Corps Headquarters were in England, doing little more than getting ready for Christmas. It was essential that he got himself and his HQ to Belgium as soon as possible. Quickly he contacted the Troop

Carrier Command and lined up every C-47 he could find. For an hour there was pandemonium at the CP, while staff officers were roused from their beds and given orders to pack ready for combat within the hour.

As the first streak of dawn began to lighten the sky, the C-47s started to roll down the runways, 55 in all, carrying Ridgway and his staff. Behind them a thick fog billowed in from the Channel. Within minutes it had covered the base. The signal light of the control tower could no longer be seen. The field was now officially 'socked in'. The Ridgway group was the last that would leave England for the next forty-eight hours. This was the last help that Hodges could expect from over the water.

2

Like grey ghosts, the refreshed SS soldiers slipped down the heights around Vieux Chateau which overlooked Stavelot and the vital bridge somewhere in the darkness below. In little groups of four and five they filed by the silent houses, keeping to the shadows, speaking only to pass on whispered orders. It was four o'clock in the morning. Peiper had begun his attack on Stavelot.

Now the first houses of the single row that led down to the bridge began to receive German 'visitors'. A startled housewife heard a soft knocking on her front door.

'Who's there?'

'Four soldiers.'

'Go away! It's still night.'

'If you don't open up,' the voice outside said, 'I'll throw a grenade in.'

The frightened woman did as she was ordered. Four young SS men entered and peered suspiciously round the candle-lit room.

The leader, who wore a soft cap decorated with a silver skull and crossbones jerked his pistol in the direction of Stavelot. 'Are there any Americans down there?'

'I don't know,' replied the frightened woman; and with that the Germans left.

Now the patrols were everywhere, searching the houses that lined the route their tanks would soon have to take, looking for Americans and information. By five they were satisfied that the houses on the approach route to the bridge were clear of Americans. A long line of tanks parked on the steep incline waited for the signal to advance.

Peiper was up and about well before dawn. In spite of his exhaustion he had not slept well. At midnight an unexpected visitor had arrived, a naval lieutenant from Skorzeny's Brigade, who had hitchhiked to the 1 SS. His news was not very encouraging. The main body of the 1 SS Division were bogged down in the mud of the Ardennes forests wherever they had taken the secondary roads and were having trouble with *Ami* resistance elsewhere. Peiper could not, therefore, expect reinforcements to reach him that day. He felt a sense of defeat, as if the 'big strike was already over'.

But that had been last night. This morning he had regained his usual drive. Looking round at the confident faces of his men, he knew that he must not let them down. They were still full of enthusiasm, strong in the knowledge that they had got the *Amis* on the run, and that they would soon be on the Meuse—perhaps even further.

He took a last glance at his map. He would take the bridge, then on through the town to the market place where he would turn west to Trois Ponts. Here he would cross the River Salm and drive westwards via Werbomont towards the Meuse. With a bit of luck he might make the river by nightfall. Kraemer's final order flashed through his mind: 'Drive hard, Peiper, and hold the reins loose.'

That was the way it should be. Jumping into his command vehicle, he told Zwigart to start up. Everywhere armoured cars and tanks did the same. The still dawn was torn apart by the roar of diesel engines. The air was full of thick blue fumes. The attack was on.

Down below in the town the Americans waited. During the night the handful of combat engineers had been reinforced by one of the units which General Hodges had 'scraped from the bottom of the barrel' during the previous evening. It was a company of the 526th Armored Infantry Battalion, under the command of Major Paul Solis with a platoon of towed 3-inch tank destroyers. Just before daybreak, Solis had got his men into position, with two platoons on the south bank of the river, a section of TDs at the roadblock, and one platoon of three 57 mm anti-tank guns and a second section of TDs in reserve around the town square to the north of the river. Now they waited, crouched by their weapons, staring nervously up at the heights from whence they knew the enemy must come.

Then they heard the roar of the tank engines, followed moments later by the clatter of metal tracks, which grew louder and louder, the noise echoing from one side of the valley to the other.

In the lead as they passed the ruins of the old castle which gave that part of Stavelot its name of Vieux Chateau, Peiper had placed his First Tank Company and Diefenthal's 3rd Grenadier Battalion. Krenser of the First Tanks had the task of rushing the bridge with his Panthers, the lightest tank in the *Kampfgruppe*, while Diefenthal's grenadiers had the job of dealing with any infantry obstruction the *Amis* might put up.

The advanced guard reached the curve in the road from where one gets a panoramic view of the town below. But on that morning the SS men had no time for the scenery. They had hardly reached the bend when the air was vent by the sound of heavy shells. Almost immediately the first vehicles were straddled by a salvo. Krenser fell badly wounded, as did several of his men. Peiper, as usual well in the lead, ordered Lieutenant Hennecke to take his place and the casualties to be taken to a nearby house. The group pushed on.

Now they could see the *Amis* down below. Hennecke did not hesitate. He ordered his first two panzers to rush the bridge at full speed, knowing in his heart that he was sending them on a suicide mission; the *Amis* would naturally have prepared the bridge for demolition. The young tank commanders, with that blind obedience which made the *Leibstandarte* what it was, set off down the hill at top speed. The first one swung round the bend. Only a matter of yards away a startled anti-tank gun crew stared at the monster in horror. Then they opened up. At that range they couldn't miss. Even the Panther's steeply-angled glacis plate did not help it. The shell crashed home. There was a great echoing clang and flames began to shoot out of the stricken vehicle.

But it did not stop. Its momentum was too great. With a rending crash it battered its way through the anti-tank obstacle and damaged two Shermans, before it finally came to rest, burning fiercely in the crisp morning air. No one got out. But the sacrifice had not been in vain.

The second Panther rattled over the little stone bridge, and the grenadiers followed in their half-tracks, dropping over the sides of the vehicles as soon as they reached the other bank and rushing for the first row of houses, in which the Americans were, firing from the hip as they went.

A wild battle began, the Americans pulling back up the narrow twisting streets that led to the centre of the town, the grenadiers at their heels all the way. With their hatches battened down, the rest of Henneck's tanks followed, rattling past the tank destroyers and anti-tank guns abandoned by their crews.

By ten o'clock the Germans had fought their way through the town and were on the road that led west towards Trois Ponts. Solis held out in the town square for a couple of hours, helped by other American units which had wandered into the town during the battle, but although he inflicted severe casualties on the advancing Germans, he simply could not stop them. In the confused fighting, he pulled what was left of his men back alone the Malmédy road instead of up the hill above Stavelot. Unwittingly he was retreating towards the great gas dump at Francorchamps.

Jochen Peiper did not wait to mop up the resistance still left at

Stavelot. In spite of the jam the naval lieutenant had reported to his rear, he was confident that the 3rd Paratroop Division would soon close up to him and take over the Stavelot situation. The easy capture of the bridge, which he had been sure the *Amis* would have prepared for demolition, had given his spirits a boost. Now he had no further time to waste on Stavelot. His eyes were set on the next town on his route, Trois Ponts, and the bridge over the Salm which would put him on the first-class road to Werbomont.

He was behind Henneck's tanks when he heard the new firing to his front. The sound told him that somewhere an American bazooka was being used. Angrily he snapped an order, and a small force of tanks detached itself from the main force and went on to search for the source of the firing.

Meanwhile Hennecke roared on towards Trois Ponts. Just as he cleared the town a group of civilians rushed to the windows of their house to look at the camouflaged tanks heading west. Hennecke's men did not hesitate. Perhaps they mistook the Belgian civilians for American soldiers, who seemed to be everywhere in the narrow winding streets of the old town. Perhaps they were just plain blood-thirsty. We shall never know. But after the chatter of the machine-gun had died away, fourteen-year-old Jose Gengoux lay in a pool of blood, shot through the stomach, and his sister Germaine sat on the kitchen floor staring bewildered at her shattered arm, which would soon have to be amputated to save her life. The first of the atrocities that would decimate the population of the little Belgian town had begun.

Solis's two remaining tank destroyers were heading east along the main highway to Malmédy, eight miles away, while Solis and what was left of his infantry were panting up a steep winding mountain road in roughly the same direction. After several miles of this, he was stopped by a Belgian officer who sprang out of a ditch immediately to his front.

Quickly the Belgian told him about the great gasoline dump, of which he and a handful of civilian workers were the sole guardians. Just then Solis heard the rumble of tanks behind him. At the foot of the hill, the first of the Panthers had begun to appear. He made a quick decision. His men were finished, and he had no anti-tank weapons, not even a bazooka, left. *But there was the gas.*

Hurriedly his men helped the Belgians to trundle five gallon jerricans out of the dump and stack them at a sharp bend in the road. Within minutes they had a fair-sized heap of cans spread out across the road, ready to be exploded as soon as the German Panzers appeared.

But their effort was in vain. The tanks did not appear. Instead they skirted the bottom of the hill and continued in a westerly direction. For a moment the little group couldn't believe their luck. The enemy hadn't seen them and the fuel dump was saved.

In later years someone was to invent the legend that the German tanks had actually attacked but had been driven off by a great barrier of flame. The U.S. Official History of the War accepted the story, as did the movies which twice featured this 'dramatic event' in their accounts of the Battle of the Bulge.

Unaware that his men had missed the vital supply dump that would have given them enough fuel to get to the Meuse and beyond, Peiper was now concentrating on the battle for the bridge at Trois Ponts.

Trois Ponts—three bridges—got its name from its two bridges over the Salm and one over the Amblève. Coming from Stavelot, the road passes under the railway line, then veers sharply to the south, crosses the Amblève, runs down a narrow valley for a couple of hundred yards and then turns west at right-angles to cross the Salm and enter the main part of the village. This road would have to be taken to get on the mainroad to Werbomont. From there he would have an almost un-obstructed path to the Meuse. But Peiper had not reckoned with four young American men named McCollum, Hollenbeck, Buchanan and Higgins.

In December, 1944, the 51st Engineer Battalion had been

given the task of cutting timber for the First Army's winter-isation and bridge timber-cutting programme. It was definitely a civilian assignment, with the battalion operating 28 civilian mills, bothered during the day with such problems as labour troubles, breakdown of machinery, transport difficulties, and

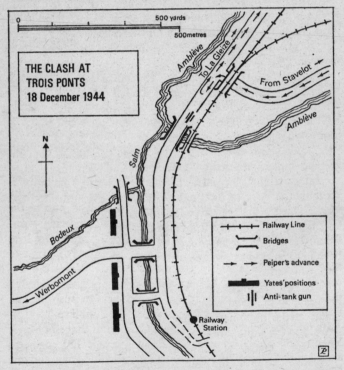

THE CLASH AT TROIS PONTS 18 December 1944

0   500 yards
     500 metres

Amblève

To La Gleize

From Stavelot

Amblève

N

Salm

Bodeux

Werbomont

	Railway Line
	Bridges
	Peiper's advance
	Yates' positions
	Anti-tank gun

Railway Station

during the evening with picking up young Belgian girls, with their long rolled hair, their clicking wooden heels and their sometimes frightening 'warmth' to their 'liberators'.

It was a good life, far from the discomfort of the front, with each of the men soon acquiring a 'little friend', to whom he went of an evening, carrying a large discreetly-wrapped package under his overcoat, which, once he was indoors, was unwrapped to the accompaniment of collective sighs of admiration of the whole family. Then there'd be the long evening, stretched out seemingly interminably by the difficulties of the language barrier, broken a little by the BBC news and the occasional glass of weak Belgian beer, before finally the family would retire to leave the young people alone, with the hurried dash back to the billets in the early hours of the next morning prior to another day 'in the office'.

But at 1730 on 17 December the idyll was shattered. The battalion was alerted to move to cover the Amblève line, blowing bridges and generally executing a delaying action. Under the command of Major Robert Yates, who had returned to the battalion as executive officer after three months in hospital, Company C was ordered to proceed to Trois Ponts and prepare to blow the bridges if necessary.

Yates arrived with an advance party just before midnight and immediately set to work getting the bridges ready for demolition. By a stroke of good luck he was at his command post at the railway station when he saw a lone anti-tank gun being towed past the window. On inquiry he found that the crew were lost, cut off from their parent unit, Company B of the 7th Armored Division's 526th Armored Infantry Battalion. Yates did not consider the legitimacy of his action; he simply commandeered the gun and its crew and ordered its members to push the gun into position forward of the bridge over the Amblève.

By the time Peiper's force crossed the river at Stavelot Major Yates' little command was ready and waiting: 120 engineers armed with 8 bazookas, four ·50 calibre machine-guns, and one 57 mm anti-tank gun, crewed by McCollum, Hollenbeck, Buchanan and Higgins. David was ready to meet Goliath.

The Germans came just before noon—nineteen Panthers, the advance guard of *Kampfgruppe* Peiper. Just in front of the underpass which led into Trois Ponts, a small group of engineers were still laying mines across the road. The tanks halted. A handful of *Pioniere* ran forward and cleared the mines, and the tanks pushed on. The first one swung under the railway line and round the corner. Before it lay the gun. The German commander gave an order. His gunner fired and missed. Then the anti-tank gun fired. A long stream of red and yellow flame shot from its muzzle. The first tank reeled. A track flopped uselessly in front of it and it came to a halt.

The next tank ground its way past its mate and opened fire. The Americans fought back desperately—the clang of the shell in the breech—eye pressed against the rubber eyepiece—a jerk at the lever—mouth open as the breech roared back and the loader was struck in the face by the hot acrid blast like being hit by a flabby fist. The clatter of the smoking shell case on to the cobbles—again the clang of the shell going into the breech and the tap of the gun commander on the loader's shoulder to indicate he could fire.

Behind the sweating crew, the engineers ran to finish their preparations to blow the bridge. Sweating in spite of the cold, they fumbled with the wires and connections, racing against the moment when the anti-tank gun must be hit.

Then the bridge was ready. Yates yelled an order. With a heavy crump, followed a second later by a great flash of yellow flame, the middle span of the bridge collapsed into the water. The demolition had been carried out in the nick of time. The leading Panther pushed on as far as it dare; then, in spite of the fire of the *Ami* anti-tank gun, took careful and deliberate aim at the sweating men only a matter of yards away. A burst of flame shot from its gun. The shell struck the little 57 mm at its base. The gun disintegrated. The four young men were killed instantly.

Peiper looked up the road from his position at the underpass and cursed those four men who lay sprawled near the ruined gun. But for them he would have taken the bridge and been on his way. As he was to say later, 'If we had captured the bridge at Trois Ponts intact and had had enough fuel, it would have been a simple matter to drive through to the River Meuse early that day.' But he controlled his anger and concentrated on his map.

Even while he did so, his men began to fall back under pressure from the engineers, who were putting up a fine stand to the left of the underpass while their comrades worked on the second bridge over the Salm which would be detonated in a few moments. Peiper saw that there was now only one possible route he could take: that to the right of the underpass, leading through the steep gorges of the Amblève to the mountain village of La Gleize, where he hoped there would be bridges to bear the weight of his 72-ton Royal Tigers. With a bit of luck he could cross the river there and get back on his Werbomont axis. The blowing of the bridge was a stroke of bad luck, but perhaps the detour would only mean that his drive to the Meuse would be delayed by a couple of hours. He packed away his map and gave the order to mount. The tanks started their engines and set off northwards at full speed. Behind them McCollum, Hollenbeck, Buchanan and Higgins stared at the sky with unseeing eyes, unaware that their sacrifice would mean that Peiper was entering a trap from which he would never escape. When he returned down this road it would be as a fugitive in the night, exhausted and starving, a beaten man.

3

It was just after breakfast on the 18th that General Hodges learned that the unidentified German armoured column which had broken through at Büllingen had passed through Stavelot and now was heading in the general direction of Spa. The news caused considerable alarm at 1st Army Headquarters. General Gavin, the first of a series of important visitors to Hodges' HQ, noted the mood immediately.

On seeing General Hodges to obtain new orders for his Division, he was not reassured. The First Army commander got down to business at once. Without pulling punches, he told the younger man that the situation south and west of Stavelot was unknown except that the enemy had evidently overrun the front positions.

Hodges had originally planned to use the 82nd at Houffalize to fill the gap between St Vith and Bastogne. But now he needed him urgently to stop the German armoured force heading west down the valley of the Amblève towards Spa. Gavin looked at the big situation map behind Hodges's shoulder and realised that if he grouped his Division around Werbomont as Hodges wanted, he would certainly block the exit channel to the north, but the southern channel between St Vith and Bastogne would be left wide open. He could see that Hodges was worried and nervous, and he went away glad to be getting back to the more familiar atmosphere of a combat command.

By mid-morning the gunfire from Trois Ponts could be heard in Spa. Its effects was to create a minor panic. Those civilians who had hesitated the night before, began to pack carpet-bags full of essentials and get on the road westwards. Soon the long road that led through the double line of pseudo-gothic hotels, where for decades nothing had ever started but many things had ended, was packed with forlorn crowds of refugees, dragging their pathetic piles of possessions behind them on little hand carts.

The sense of panic transferred itself also to the lobby of the Hotel Britannica. The 'canteen commandos', as the front-line GIs called the rear-echelon clerks, began to throw anxious glances through the tall french windows of the hotel, as if they expected the first of the enemy panzers to come barrelling down the steep hill into the town at any moment.

Hodges' next visitor was Major-General Lawton Collins, commander of VII Corps. 'Nice to see you, Joe,' he said, 'Big Simp[1] is letting me borrow you until we straighten out this mess down here. The Germans have broken through all along the front.'

---

[1] General Simpson, commander of the US 9th Army, which was stationed further north.

At that moment, there was a knock at the door. 'Monk' Dickson came in, greeted General Collins briefly and said: 'General, if you don't want to get captured you'd better get out of town! The Germans are only a mile away.'

Hodges grinned. 'Later, later,' he said vaguely. In the silence that followed the rumble of artillery and the faint crackle of what might have been small arms fire could be heard in the distance.

Dickson tried again: 'But General, there is no time to lose!'

Hodges raised a pale hand and waved his intelligence officer out of the room, 'Hm, Joe,' he cleared his throat, 'you're going to be my strategic reserve . . . '

By midday on the 18th, Hodges's little joke seemed almost to be coming true. The barrel was about scraped clean on the Continent, and at Eisenhower's headquarters at Versailles they had just learned that England was fogged in. They could expect neither air support nor the delivery of the only reinforcements left in the United Kingdom.

That morning, just as at Spa, the mood at the Petit Trianon Palace slumped to zero. Now after the German offensive had been going for forty-eight hours, the members of the enormous 5,000 man HQ began to realise how overconfident they had been refusing even to consider the possibility that the enemy would ever again be able to assemble enough strength to attack them after the débâcle in France in the summer of 1944. Already Intelligence had identified some twenty odd German divisions, over a third of them armoured.

General Eisenhower, who like his staff officers had failed to believe that the Germans could ever again launch an attack on the American front and had consequently failed to build up a reserve for this eventuality, finally came to the conclusion that this was an all-out attack. Admittedly his initial decision to hold the flanks of the enemy's point of penetration was sound. The two shoulders to left and right of the German attack were holding and resistance was firm at the vital communication points. But he had been slow to realise just how badly Hodges' army had been hit. Now there was a huge gap where Middleton's VIII Corps had once been, into which what reserves he had were being poured piecemeal, without any apparent overall plan.

Eisenhower sat alone in his big office overlooking the courtyard where nearly a quarter of a century before the 'Old Men of Europe' had walked up and down planning those Versailles decisions which were to lay the foundations of a new war. In the end he made up his mind. He would call off General Patton's Saar offensive scheduled to start on the 19th. Patton's men would counter-attack against the Germans in the Bulge. Tomorrow he would get together with Bradley and Patton at Verdun, where they would work out the details.

By the time Eisenhower had made his decision to meet Patton, the German Radio had begun to boom out the first important details of the new offensive. For the first time for many months, the loudspeakers trembled with the bombastic brass of the military band which in the good days of the early forties had heralded a major victory virtually every other day. Now those enthusiastic, fast-speaking announcers of the great days were back, their voices trembling with emotion as they cried to crowds gathered round the 'people's receiver' in factory, *gasthaus*, school and home: *'Our troops march again . . . We shall present the Leader with Antwerp for Christmas . . . The Anglo-Americans are reeling back everywhere . . . Already we have achieved major breakthroughs on the Ardennes front.'*

And at his headquarters, a suddenly revived Hitler promised his entourage that Peiper would have the oak leaves to his Knight's Cross of the Iron Cross for this. Peiper was living up fully to the great expectations the Fuehrer had placed in the young SS commander.

If there were faint-hearts at Allied headquarters that day, General Matthew Ridgway was not one of them. In spite of the dense fog, he had landed safely at the airport at Rheims and learning there that his two airborne divisions had set off for the Ardennes, ordered the driver of the waiting car to follow them, heading in the general direction of Bastogne where Middleton had his headquarters. At Rheims no one knew much about the situation except that it was very confused. Confusion did not worry Ridgway. As an airborne commander who had gone through the terrible mess of the pre-dawn landing in Normandy, he was used to it.

By late afternoon, First Army was beginning to evacuate Spa. The sound of firing grew louder. A rumour fled through the frantically-packing soldiers that the Germans were less than two thousand yards away. A light plane had got under the cloud base and spotted the first enemy vehicles. It was followed a little later by another and more terrifying rumour—the Germans were SS men. A paybook had been picked up from a dead body at Stavelot identifying the German armoured formation. The headquarters men swallowed hard, their minds full of what had happened at Malmédy the day before, and redoubled their efforts.

When darkness fell, apart from a few staff officers, the flight from Spa had been completed. Up in his office Hodges packed his important papers in his briefcase and walked calmly to the waiting staff car, striding through the big salon on the second floor where, twenty-five years before, Kaiser Wilhelm the Second had finally recognised his defeat and signed his abdication. The car drove off at once.

Now the Americans were gone. The commander of an army of 300,000 men had been forced to flee before a handful of German troops. The town lay open for the taking.

4

Peiper had had an easy passage to La Gleize. There was al-most no opposition and his tanks reached the village in good time in spite of the twisting hilly road. Reaching the village, a collection of small stone houses grouped around the little church, the most prominent building being the grandiose

Château du Froide Cour, he sent out a reconnaissance group to check his front. They returned almost immediately to tell him that they had succeeded in capturing a bridge just over a mile to the southwest of the town at the village of Cheneux. Using this bridge he could get back on the Werbomont road that had been denied to him at Trois Ponts.

Hurriedly he got his force back on the road again towards Cheneux. But here bad luck struck him once more. He had just cleared the bridge himself when four Thunderbolt fighter-bombers came roaring in at almost tree-top level. Violet lights crackled along the planes' wings. The valley was filled with the roar of their engines. The Germans leaped from their vehicles and ran frantically for cover. Then the bombs came—five-hundred pounders. Lying in a ditch, his face in the dirt, Peiper cursed bitterly until the heaving earth rose under the impact of a bomb and filled his mouth with earth.

American planes were bombing the whole twenty-mile length of the column as it lay stretched out between Lodemez on the road from Ligneuville through Stavelot, past Trois Ponts and on to Cheneux. Guided by Piper Cubs of the 109th Tactical Reconnaissance Squadron, planes from the 365th Fighter Group swept in from the direction of La Gleize and struck the helpless Germans trapped on the winding mountain roads. For two hours they circled the German column. Here and there the mobile *Vierling* flak opened up and fought back for a little while. But soon their crews fled into the woods or into the cellars of nearby houses.

This first bombing shook up the column badly, especially those members of it who had only served in Russia and had not undergone the Allied air attacks of the Normandy battles. They and the younger men were nervous and tense as they returned to their vehicles and started to crawl forward once more, keeping a wary eye on the darkening sky. In particular, the soldiers of the 7th Tank Companies now moving through Stavelot were affected by the sudden attack. As they manoeuvred their way round the awkward bends they fired their machine guns indiscriminately at anything that moved. Just as they were leaving the town one of the great 72-ton Royal Tigers stopped outside the house of Monsieur Lambert, named *Les Quartiers*, and two SS soldiers descended, pistols in hand, and hammered on the wooden door. Lambert went to the door, opened it and faced them. One of them shot him without a word, stepped over his body and entered the hall, calling 'Are there any Americans here?'

Madame Lambert, who had heard the shot but did not realise that it was her husband who had been killed, came out of the kitchen and faced the murderers, followed by her young daughter Claudine. The young men demanded beer and, trembling with fear, Madame Lambert hurried away to fetch it, leaving her daughter facing them alone. It was only when she returned with the drink that Madame Lambert became aware of her husband lying still in a pool of blood across his own threshold.

The man who had murdered him saw the direction of her gaze, laughed and seizing the drink out of her hand, drained it in a gulp. Then he swaggered out, not even looking at the murdered man as he stepped over him.

A second atrocity had been committed at Stavelot. It was a portent of what was to come.

The bombing had cost Peiper two hours and ten vehicles. He was angry and impatient. He snapped out an order and got the column moving again. He was on the road heading towards Werbomont, eight or nine kilometres away, but protected in part by the Lienne, a small yet unfordable river. He hoped that he would find the bridge at the hamlet of Neufmoulin still intact.

At the café opposite the bridge a platoon of combat engineers from the 291st Combat Engineer Battalion were hastily sorting out their explosives. It was too dark to do the job outside. As they ran outside to the bridge they could hear the rattle and clatter of tanks on the other side of the hill. A sergeant waded into the icy water up to his waist and began to attach the explosives. Another man ran across the bridge and did the same on the other side of the span. The sound was getting nearer and nearer as the column roared on.

But it arrived too late. Just as the first vehicle topped the rise the bridge went up in a spectacular cloud of dust, rubble and violent flame. Peiper cursed. His road westwards was blocked once more. He turned back the way he had come.

At about the same time as the Neufmoulin bridge was blown up, a small column of German half-tracks was making its way cautiously along the road which ran to the right of the Lienne Creek. It had found a bridge intact, which, although it was too light to bear the Royal Tigers, would bear the weight of the half-tracks. Now the task was to find another bridge which would stand the 72-ton weight of the big tanks.

Strung out at one hundred metres, distance, the half-tracks rattled down the road, their crews peering through the growing darkness, eyes only for the water to their left. They did not see the men crouched on the ridge to their right until it was too late. Suddenly there was the thump of a bazooka, and in a shower of angry sparks the projectile struck the first half-track a resounding whack. Flames shot up immediately from the German vehicle.

At once small arms fire began to crackle along the ridge. Another bazooka fired and a second half-track skidded to a halt and burst into flames. Hastily the crew baled out and returned the fire. But not for long. When in quick succession, a third, fourth and fifth half-track was struck and set on fire, what was left of the German column turned and headed back the way it had come.

On the ridge the soldiers were excited in spite of the exhaustion of a long day's ride in open trucks. They were pleased with the results of their first brush with the enemy, and they shouted joking comments to one another as they lay in the shallow holes they had hastily shovelled an hour or so before. Now they relaxed, tilting back their heavy helmets and lighting their first cigarettes.

1. Obersturmbannfuehrer
   Jochen Peiper

2. Major Hal McCown

3. Lieutenant Lyle Bouck

4. Peter Rupp

5 and 6. Peiper reads a signpost (above) and checks his map (below)

Standing on the ridge, their commander stared down at them proudly. It was his first battalion command and West Pointer Major Hal McCown wanted to make a success of it. He hadn't been too sure of his new battalion up to now, but the men—many of them replacements—had done a good job of work. Looking at them, McCown felt he could rely on the 2nd Battalion of the 119th Infantry. Then he went back to the job of interrogating the sole prisoner they had taken—a sullen youth from the 2nd SS Panzer Grenadiers. Regimental headquarters, hastily settling in somewhere to the rear, would be glad of all the intelligence it could get, he imagined. About him the tired men extinguished their cigarettes and began to make themselves as comfortable as they could for the night.

5

The 30th Infantry Division, which had just had its first brush with Peiper, was called 'Old Hickory', because it had been raised in South Carolina, birthplace of Andrew Jackson who had borne this nickname on account of his toughness and endurance. The Thirtieth Division was a veteran organisation. Under its, 52-year-old commander, General Leland Hobbs, who belonged to the famous West Point Class of '15, which numbered Eisenhower and Bradley among its numbers, it had proved itself in Normandy in August, 1944. That month it had stood in the way of a desperate four-division German counter-attack, which had tried to break through to the coast and cut off Patton's Third Army galloping across Brittany through the narrow Avranches corridor. The Mortain counter-attack had nearly decimated the Division, but it had shown its worth, especially around Hill 617 and earned itself another nickname, this time from the Germans. It was 'Roosevelt's Butchers'.

During the Mortain counter-attack, one of the German formations which had struck the thin over-extended 30th Division line had been the *Leibstandarte Adolf Hitler*. Now

'Roosevelt's Butchers' were to meet the same enemy again and this time it would be a struggle to the death.

The events of that late afternoon seemed to indicate to Hobbs that his division was going to be as successful defending the Amblève River Line as it had been at Mortain some four months earlier. After the initial good news of McCown's exploits at the Lienne came in, further reports followed from the 1st Battalion of the 117th Infantry on the heights above Stavelot.

Circling the town cautiously by way of Francorchamps, the battalion, under the command of Colonel Ernest Frankland, bumped into the fleeing TDs of the 526th Infantry. The scared crews told him they were the 'last survivors' and advised him that Stavelot was 'crawling with Krauts'. Frankland ignored the information and pushed on till, sometime in the middle of the afternoon, he made contact with Major Solis, where he de-trucked his infantry near the gasoline roadblock.

Frankland was determined to attack and capture Stavelot at once, in spite of the fact he had no artillery support. However, he did have a platoon of towed 3-inch tank-destroyers. They would have to suffice.

His lead companies, A and B, operating abreast, thrust forward rapidly. Reaching the edge of the town, they were just about to deploy when ten German tanks, returning hastily from Trois Ponts, counter-attacked. But luck was on the Americans' side. Just at this moment the fighter-bombers of IX Tactical Air Command chose to strike again. The Thunderbolts came zooming down, the red-flamed rockets hurtling towards the tanks. The Germans scuttled for cover.

Frankland urged his men on, putting into practice the technique of house-to-house fighting they had studied so often in battle school: the mad dash forward under the cover of machine-gun fire—the pause at the house door—a grenade through the window—head down as it exploded, sending fragments of glass shooting out of the shattered window—the foot against the suddenly sagging door—a burst of fire from the 'burp gun'—then in! The hectic scramble through the still-smoking rooms, littered with the pathetic debris of a once peaceful home—and occasionally the dead and dying bodies of German soldiers sprawled out among the rubble.

By evening Frankland's men had cleared half the town and had tied in with the 2nd Battalion of the 117th Infantry Regiment located between Stavelot and Malmédy. But the Germans still held the bridge and its approaches, with a Tiger tank on the far side of the river, hidden behind a house, withstanding all their efforts to knock it out. In the end, as it grew close to midnight, the 1st Battalion gave up. Now the night grew quiet save for the occasional chatter of the obstinate Tiger's machine-gun. The 1st Battalion had had enough for that day.

Up the steep road from La Gleize, another battalion of the 30th Infantry Division waited for Peiper at the hill village of Stoumont. It was the 3rd Battalion of the 119th Infantry, commanded by Colonel Roy Fitzgerald, who had taken over the little village schoolhouse just near the church on the main road as his command post. Colonel Fitzgerald knew that he had drawn the key assignment of the regiment. The enemy had been frustrated everywhere in his attempt to break out of the Amblève vally to the west. Now there was only Stoumont left, the sole remaining exit for the Germans, and he had just been told that the enemy was massing only one and a half miles away at La Gleize.

Fitzgerald studied his map in the old-fashioned one-room schoolhouse. His battalion was strung out in a hastily-drawn-up line to north, south and east of the village, with a handful of towed 3-inch tank-destroyers and three 57 mm anti-tank guns as sole artillery support against a tank attack, plus two 90 mm anti-aircraft guns which might be employed as anti-tank weapons at a pinch. It wasn't much to stop an armoured division. Admittedly to his rear the regiment's 1st Battalion was located some three miles away near the Regimental Commander, Colonel Sutherland's CP. But that was it. There was nothing else between the Germans and the troopers of the 82nd Airborne who were, as Sutherland had informed him, expected to arrive somewhere around Werbomont during the night. The situation certainly didn't look too good.

In the corner of the room where for years he had taught generations of Stoumont children, Monsieur Ernest Natalis, a thin, erect man in his late forties with a trace of a moustache under his long nose, watched the scene with almost academic interest. Monsieur Natalis, the village teacher, was always avid for information, eager to improve himself in spite of the fact that he had a settled position for which no new knowledge was really necessary. One of the teacher's hobbies was learning foreign languages. Apart from his native French and Flemish, he spoke fluent German and English, as well as three or four other languages. Now, completely divorced from the significance of the scene, concerned only with the language, he listened to the English of the American officers, mentally noting the grammatical mistakes and the slang usages, as if he were preparing to censure one of his pupils for the use of a Walloon dialect word instead of correct French.

But as the evening wore on, Natalis forgot his linguistic interests. He became absorbed in observing a process completely new to him: men at war in a situation which was getting progressively worse—messengers passing in and out of the room, rifles slung over their shoulders, bringing reports that became steadily more pessimistic. There were enemy paratroopers in the hills north of the town. The movement of tanks had been reported in La Gleize. Patrols had been seen making their way up the steep road to Stoumont . . . Thus it went on, with more and more red marks being drawn on the map overlay, and the mood in the little CP sinking deeper and deeper accordingly.

Finally Colonel Fitzgerald turned to his staff and said quietly and slowly in an English that the little man in the shabby civilian clothes in the corner could hear and understand distinctly: 'Gentlemen, it looks as if we may all be prisoners by tomorrow morning.'

Now silence began to decend upon the Amblève River

battlefield. From Stavelot to Stoumont the gunfire died away. Here and there a flare hushed into the night sky and bathed everything in its icy light; but that was all.

Up at his headquarters in the Château du Froide Cour, Peiper reviewed the day. It had had its big disappointments for him, with bridges being blown in front of his nose all along the line of the Amblève, and the evening situation report told him his column was getting pretty low on fuel again. Yet all the same he had not suffered any great losses in men or material during the day's fighting. Around La Gleize he had a virtually intact mixed battalion of Mark IVs and Panthers, supported by Diefenthal's grenadiers, plus a company of the 3rd Paratroopers. In addition, a little to his rear, he had another battalion of Tigers, a battalion of mobile flak and a battery of 105 mm self-propelled guns. It was a formidable force of two thousand odd men and perhaps two hundred armoured vehicles.

His men, too, were in good spirits, in spite of everything. As he had walked round their lines earlier in the evening, and chatted to them of the attack he would launch on Stoumont the next morning, they had responded eagerly and he knew he could rely on them. Men of a half-a-dozen different nationalities, yet all of pure aryan blood, they looked tired admittedly, but still young, strong and, above all, confident in the value of their mission for the German Fatherland. Tomorrow they would get to the Meuse.

The Defence

BOOK TWO
The Defence

Day Four:
TUESDAY, 19 DECEMBER, 1944

'All you people here in this region are terrorists!'

Jochen Peiper to
M. Natalis, Stoumont.

General Ridgway, at Bastogne, woke early on the morning of 19 December and wasted little time washing and dressing. The headquarters staff of VIII Corps had not impressed him the night before. Middleton had been his old, somewhat slow self, calm and plodding, the typical infantryman; but his staff had been fraught with pessimism and foreboding. The Corps' 106th Division was finished, as was the 14th Cavalry; the 28th Infantry Division had taken bad losses and now the Corps' communications to the front had been cut so that HQ seemed completely in the dark. Gloom had dominated his discussions with the Corps staff the previous evening and he was glad to be getting out of Bastogne and back to his own Corps. As soon as he had had a cup of coffee and spoken to Middleton once more, he would hit the road, fog or no fog, and set up his own CP a little to the south of Gavin's 82nd Airborne at Werbomont—perhaps at Trois Ponts.

As he walked along the dark corridor in search of breakfast he could not help overhearing the conversation of two private soldiers some way behind him.

The one said: 'We'd better get the hell out of here.'

The other answered in a resigned tone: 'We can't. They've got us surrounded.'

On that foggy December morning, the mood of the two privates at Middleton's HQ was reflected everywhere in the Allied high command. The Ardennes counter-attack had caught the Allies with their pants down and their reaction was one of amazement and incredulity. They had convinced themselves for months that the Germans were finished, almost on the point of collapse. Victory, they had been telling one another, was just round the corner. But by 19 December the mood had changed to one of panic and fear.

Everywhere communications were broken. Rumour was rampant. Saboteurs and paratroopers were miles behind the Allied lines. The American front was 'bugging out'. Doubt and confusion spread rapidly in the rear areas. Cooks and clerks were given rifles and put in hastily-established strongpoints. Puzzled negroes from the COMZ transport units were told they were now riflemen. Replacement centres were ordered to form provisional regiments for immediate employment against the German armour expected to break through at any moment. And everywhere in the rear areas, the clerks and administrators began to burn secret documents and prepare the long line of waiting trucks for the dash to the French coast.

It was against this background of near-panic and defeatism that the Supreme Commander, General Eisenhower, raced through northern France that morning to arrive in Verdun at eleven o'clock. After him, as he entered the bitterly cold squadroom in the former French Army *Maginot Caserne*, filed some of the top American commanders: Bradley, Patton, Devers and Eisenhower's own chief-of-staff, sour-faced General Bedell Smith. With a noisy shuffle of wooden chairs, they took their places.

Eisenhower, his usual grin gone, opened the proceedings, looking round at the semi-circle of brass. 'The present situation is to be regarded as one of opportunity,' he began with false optimism, 'and not one of disaster.' He paused and his face spread in that famous smile that had endeared him to thousands of Allied citizens and would one day win him a vital election. 'There will be only cheerful faces at this conference table.'

Then General Strong, Eisenhower's chief intelligence officer, stepped forward and began to brief them on the situation in the Ardennes at 0900 that morning.

The details of the Verdun Conference are well known. Indeed it is usually regarded as the turning point in the Battle of the Bulge, for it showed that the Supreme Commander had at last recognised the seriousness of the German threat and was taking measures to counter that threat. When the Conference broke up in the early afternoon, it had been decided that General Patton's Third Army would disengage itself from the battle in the Saar and launch an attack on the German southern flank in the Ardennes by, at the latest, 23 December.

As they left the Conference together, Eisenhower turned to Patton, and pointing to his new fifth star, remarked, 'It's a funny thing but every time I get another star I get attacked.' 'Yeah,' replied Patton, 'and every time you get attacked I have to bail you out.' In this jovial mood, the two men parted, confident that the situation was now under control.

But the Supreme Commander would not have been so confident if he could have seen his Amblève Front at the moment. It was ablaze from end to end. At Stavelot an all-out German attack was underway, with Frankland's battalion of infantry facing a whole panzer grenadier regiment. Under the command of *Obersturmbannfuehrer* Sandig, the 2nd SS Panzer Grenadier Regiment, which was Peiper's running mate in the *Leibstandarte*, was making a desperate attempt to clear Stavelot and break through to the Division's leading element at La Gleize.

The attack started at noon. Covered by intensive mortar and machine-gun fire, which kept Frankland's men cowering in the shattered houses near the river, six Tiger tanks began to rumble towards the vital bridge. At the same time a dozen or so amphibious vehicles plumped into the river a hundred yards away.

But during the night Colonel Frankland's command had been reinforced by a battery of artillery. Located on the heights overlooking the town, it now crashed into action. It was not a moment too soon. The first salvo missed and great spouts of water shot thirty feet in the air. The second salvo was dead on target. Some boats disintegrated completely. Others plunged under the water. Suddenly the river was full of dead and dying, and panic-stricken, heavily-laden SS men fighting for their lives in the fast-running stream. The third salvo was also on target and the last of the little boats went under. The river crossing had failed.

But Colonel Sandig still had his Tigers, and now as the first one approached the bridge the GIs watched with fascinated horror. Their heaviest weapon was the ·30 calibre machine-gun. Just as the German tank was about to cross the bridge, a TD from the platoon Frankland had brought with him, rumbled up and came to a halt where the steep road from the bridge goes into a gentle curve. Quickly the crew lined the German tank up in their lens. Before the Tiger could react, the tank-destroyer fired. The great 90 mm shell hit the Tiger between its deck and turret, where its armour was easiest to penetrate. There was a dull muffled explosion from within the tank. Then the hatch cover flew off to be followed a moment later by a brilliant flash of red and yellow light. Smoke began to pour from the open turret. It came to an abrupt halt on the German side of the river. None of the crew got out. The remaining Tigers fled for cover, their engines in low gear, kicking up a devil of a row. It was over for the time being.

But while one danger had been averted, another was looming up in the west. Earlier that morning Peiper had learned of the threat to his communications, posed by the *Amis* in Stavelot. He summoned Major Knittel, who commanded the rear element at La Gleize, and ordered him to turn his reconnaissance battalion about and attack Stavelot. Knittel, whose command consisted of a few tanks, light armoured vehicles and some mobile artillery, nodded in understanding. Just before he left, however, he said in a low voice, '*Die haben 'n ganze Menge auf der Kreuzung umgelegt*'.[1]

---

[1] 'They've killed a good few at the crossroads.'

'*The crossroads?*' Peiper asked, looking up from his map.

'Yes, the one at the turn-off to Engelsdorf (Ligneuville). There's a lot of *Amis* dead there.'

Peiper did not know it then but Knittel had given him the first news of what the world would one day call 'The Mamédy Massacre'.

At midday Knittel's reconnaissance battalion went into action to the west of Stavelot. The Major took up his headquarters at a burned-out farm just outside Trois Ponts. Here he quickly divided his command into two. One half under Captain Koblenz was to advance to Stavelot along the road which ran to the north of the River Amblève, while the other under the command of Captain Goltz was to take a steep winding secondary road that led to the hill villages of Ster, Parfondruy and Renardmont, from whence they would be sufficiently elevated to take the troublesome *Ami* battery behind Stoumont under counterfire.

The American forward artillery observers soon spotted Koblenz's column as it moved down the valley road, hemmed in by the river to the right and the steep hillside to the left. A hail of gunfire immediately rained down on the helplessly exposed Germans and within a matter of minutes the advance had come to an end.

The Americans then turned their attention on Goltz who had succeeded in advancing as far as the three villages, where the surprised inhabitants had run out to meet them, wide grins on their faces thinking they were Americans. Their smiles did not last long.

Again the deadly barrage descended. The first salvoes landed directly on target. Germans fell dead and wounded everywhere. An ammunition-box was hit and exploded in a massive flash of violent light. Goltz's advance had come to an equally abrupt halt.

By mid-afternoon the reports started to come back to Knittel's HQ in the cellars of the burned-out farm. His regiment had suffered very bad casualties—three hundred killed and wounded, more than a third of his force, and both Koblenz and Goltz still pinned down by artillery. A mood of bitterness and despair began to make itself felt as the casualty reports kept coming in.

2

The killing began without warning. In spite of the battle raging outside and the clatter of German armour on the road that ran before his house, M. Tony Lambert-Bock decided to have a shave. All morning he had been in the cellar with his family and others who had sought refuge in his house. Now it was 2 pm and still he was unwashed and unshaved; and M. Lambert-Bock was a stickler for a neat appearance. Despite the warnings of his family, he decided it was time for his toilette. He was busy shaving his face in cold water when he heard the front door burst open. Thinking that the blast of exploding shells might have forced it, he left the bathroom, face still half-covered with lather, to close it. Suddenly his razor dropped from his fingers. A group of armed SS men stood before him. Without a word one of them strode across the hall and shot M. Lambert-Bock in the head. He dropped without a sound and the SS men clumped out.

In the cellar the others heard the shot but they were afraid to go and see what had happened. At length M. Lambert-Bock's son ventured up the stairs; he was back within moments. '*Ils ont tué mon papa*,' he cried.

The massacre was under way.

An hour later five German soldiers entered the house occupied by M. and Mme Georgin, Mme Counet, and the Nicolay family. Without a word, two of them went upstairs while the other three, armed with machine pistols, herded the occupants into the kitchen. Suddenly one of the three shouted, 'You've being hiding bandits here!'

The terrified Belgians knew what he meant. 'No,' they cried, 'we have had no Americans here. *Not one!*'

The soldiers were not appeased. One of them ordered Louis

Nicolay to follow him outside. Nicolay did as he was told. For a moment there was silence in the little kitchen. Then the silence was shattered by a single shot. Madame Nicolay began to weep.

One of the remaining Germans now beckoned M. Georgin to follow him. Automatically Georgin followed the SS man to the door. But his brain was racing. He was not going to suffer the same fate as Nicolay—to be slaughtered like some dumb animal. The German indicated to Georgin he should walk on past him. There was a click; Georgin took a deep breath; then summoning up all of his energy, he broke away, pelting across the cobbles towards the river. For what seemed an age, the German failed to react. Then there was a sudden bellow of rage, followed by a burst of bullets. Georgin dropped immediately. He hit the *pavé* with a crash. Trembling all over, he held his breath and hoped they would think he was dead. The man standing at the door of the house must have thought so, for he turned and went back into the house.

Georgin gave himself five minutes. Then cautiously, centimetre by centimetre, he began to crawl to the river bank. Finally he made it; he dropped into the river and struck out. Just as he was clambering up the far bank a machine-gun opened up and he fell heavily, his arm nearly severed by German bullets.[1]

Now there was shooting all along the road that ran between Stavelot and Trois Ponts, and in the hamlets above the road the situation was no different. Four civilians were shot in Ster and fifteen outside it. At Renardmont nineteen were slaughtered and their houses set on fire to hide the crime. In Parfondruy twenty-six were killed. At the Hurlet Farm, just outside the village, a dozen people were mown down by SS men armed with a machine-gun. When they had gone and the frightened villagers crept out of their hiding places they found among the dead, whose ages ranged from 9 month old Bruno Klein-Terf to seventy-eight year old Josephine Grosjean-Hourand, a single

---

[1] M. Georgin was luckier than his wife and the rest of the people in the house. They were found several days later, shot dead.

survivor. Two year old Monique Thonon was still alive, covered in blood as she lay at the side of her mother.

All afternoon the killings went on. Dusk fell and still they continued. Everywhere the young SS men (they were mostly teenagers who committed the murders), frustrated in their attempt to push westwards and battered continually by the American artillery, burst into the little houses along the river bank, crying the two sentences which were their justification for what was to follow: 'You are hiding Americans! They have been firing upon us!' Then they would start shooting. The number of dead civilians in the hill hamlets and along the Stavelot–Trois Ponts road mounted rapidly.

Just before Koblenz's force had launched its attack along the Stavelot road, a Mme Régine Grégoire, who had been born Régine Heuser at Manderfeld near the border and spoke fluent German, decided to take her two children and seek refuge in the cellar of M. Legaye's house, which was opposite her own. There she found a crowd of frightened refugees already gathered. With herself and her two children, there were twenty-six people, mostly women and children.

Nothing happened all afternoon save that a lone GI came in and stared wordlessly around at the frightened faces, as if he were looking for someone. He went away and they settled down again to wait out the battle.

It grew dark. The women fed the children bread and the stiff smoked bacon, which is a speciality of that part of Belgium. Another American soldier came in, armed with a rifle. Using a mixture of sign language, a few words of French and carefully pronounced English, he told the little group of civilians that the Germans were attacking the nearby hamlet of Ster and that the best they could do was to remain in the cellar until it was all over. He left and the women started putting the small children on the bucket in the corner prior to settling them down for the night. It was now six o'clock.

Suddenly a shot rang out just above their heads, then a volley. It was answered by another volley further away. The firing grew

7. A Royal Tiger tank advancing through a forest

8. The U.S. Air Force knocked out this Tiger tank just outside Bastogne

9. The bridge at Malmédy mined for demolition

10. Malmédy, after the third Allied air raid, 25 December, 1944

more intense. It settled into a regular routine. Shots above their heads, followed moments later by others in the distance. A machine-gun began firing. Another joined in. A miniature battle was developing above them.

After about an hour the battle stopped as abruptly as it had started. The firing died away and the terrified civilians in the cellar waited for the next shock. It came quickly enough. The door was suddenly flung open and a hard object came tumbling down the cellar steps. For one moment the civilians stared at it in bewilderment. Then they flung themselves to all sides, faces buried in arms. It was a grenade! There was a crack, a brisk flash of violet flame and metal shreds flew through the room. Miraculously no one was hurt.

A few moments later another grenade followed. Mme Grégoire felt an intense pain in her leg. She looked down. A piece of metal had ripped through her dark woollen stocking. She was bleeding slightly.

Up above a harsh voice cried. '*Hieraus!*'

Then panic broke out in the cellar. Someone knew that Mme Grégoire spoke German, and they cried to her, 'Tell them we're all civilians here!'

She did as she was told, but all she got in reply was the harsh voice above crying once again, '*Raus!*'

Taking her children firmly by the hand, she climbed the stairs to be met by half-a-dozen SS men. Mme Grégoire looked at their wild young faces and saw that one wrong move would suffice to start them shooting. Hurriedly she repeated the information that there were only women and children in the cellar plus two old men.

More SS men came up; she was cross-examined in a mixture of German and French, then satisfied, the leader of the young soldiers, a sergeant not much older than the teenagers he commanded, told her to get the rest of the people in the cellar up.

She did as she was told. The frightened women and children filed out and were directed through Mme Grégoire to go into the garden of the little house, and sit or crouch in a row near the hedge. Hurriedly the Belgians did as they were told.

The sergeant turned to Mme Grégoire and told her to look after a 'comrade' who had been shot in the fight that had raged above their heads. Obediently, still accompanied by her two terrified children, she crossed the room and looked at the wounded soldier who was lying on a couch. He was bleeding badly from a gunshot wound. She looked around for something to mop up the blood. The man who had thrown the grenade handed her a field dressing. 'One of the civilians here shot at us,' he said angrily looking down at her.

'That's not true,' she replied hotly, 'It's you who wounded one of us with your grenade.'

'Don't shout at me like that!' he cried and kicked her. With that he went away and left her to her job. But she didn't continue it for very long. Suddenly the house echoed with shots again. Mme Grégoire looked up from her task. Two young soldiers, armed with a revolver and a rifle, were systematically shooting the people crouched near the hedge. One after another, they were dragged before the executioners and shot—Prosper Legaye (aged 66), his wife Marie Crismer (63), his two daughters Jeanne (aged 40) and Alice (39), his granddaughter Marie Jeanne (9), Octaviell Lecoq (68), Henri Daisomont (52), who had sworn two days before he would never again flee his native town, his wife and his two daughters, Anne-Marie (18) and Marie-Thérèse (14), Rouxhet (41), her children, Roland (14), Marc (12), Monique (9) and Bruno (7).

They were followed by Mme Prince (42), who cried out just before she was shot, 'My poor children without a mother!' As she fell, her three children were also dragged to their feet and followed her to their deaths—Yvon (14), Elisa (12) and Pol (4). One after another, they were shot—Mme Lecoq (60), her daughter Jeanne (20), Madame Rémy (32), her son Jean (8) . . .

Finally the firing stopped and Mme Grégoire turned in anguish to the soldier standing beside her. 'There was nobody here but innocent civilians', she cried.

The soldier shrugged. 'The innocent must pay for those who are guilty. The people of Stavelot have been harbouring American soldiers.'

With that she was led away to a cellar in another house where she remained until she was freed a few days later. She was the only survivor of those who had taken refuge in the cellar of M. Legaye's house.

In the end some 130 civilians were killed in and around Stavelot that day; forty-seven women, twenty-three children and sixty men. By the evening of the 19th there was not a family in the town that had not lost a member.

What can one say of such things? Admittedly some of the murders were committed in the genuine belief that the local populace had fired upon the Germans, although Colonel Peiper admitted after the war that his men never encountered a single Belgian sharp-shooter during the whole operation.[1] A few deaths probably caused by artillery fire were later ascribed to the infantry. Yet one need only look at photographs of some of the victims taken immediately after the battle to see that they had been killed by small arms fire at close range.

3

The German attack on Stoumont started just after dawn. Three Tigers came rattling down the road at full speed, firing as they went. Behind them to left and right was a skirmish line of infantry. Before the Americans could fire a shot, the leading tank was through the first roadblock, the next followed, and the next and then the infantry were on top of the Americans.

The defence broke almost immediately. There was no hesitation, no sidling to the rear. They sprang out of their holes

---

[1] In a conversation with the author, Colonel Peiper stated that Corporal Edmund Tomczak, wounded and left behind in Stavelot, was threatened by a mob of Belgian civilians, armed with shotguns. As far as Peiper could recollect this was the only armed resistance they encountered on the part of civilians.

and pelted down the cobbled road towards the village. The Germans overtook them easily and they surrendered in their scores.

Desperately the two anti-aircraft guns tried to take a bearing on the advancing Germans, but fog was rolling in and they couldn't see more than fifty yards beyond their weapon pits. They called for flares over their radio, but none came, and they gave up.

Now the Germans were rolling up the company located on the eastern side of the village. It broke and started to retreat, uncovering the eight towed tank-destroyers. Their crews joined the infantry. Minutes later all eight were in German hands without a shot having been fired. Quickly the Germans pressed down the hill into the village itself. Two anti-aircraftmen, Privates Seamon and Darago, who had had five minutes instruction in how to use a bazooka just before the attack started, took up their positions with the unfamiliar weapons and waited for the Germans to come. They did not have to wait long. A small group of Tigers soon emerged from the fog ahead of them. The artillerymen fired and missed. They fired again. There was a resounding clang of metal on metal. One tank came to an abrupt halt and begun to burn. They fired a third time and stopped another tank.

But the attack was not to be stopped by such isolated examples of individual bravery. Frankland's rifle company to the south of the town was cut off and the one inside the town was wiped out. The third company did not wait for orders. Withdrawing under cover of smoke they tumbled down the hill towards the positions held by their sister battalion, the First.

By noon Stoumont was in German hands and Fitzgerald's battalion in full retreat with most of its heavy equipment abandoned or destroyed and some 267 of its men dead or taken prisoner.

The Germans went from house to house searching for Americans. Monsieur Natalis, who had now seen the realisation of Colonel Frankland's prediction of the night before, was horrified at the way the Germans were behaving. Leaving his friend Doctor Robinson's house, where he had sheltered during the attack, he found a dying American soldier in the gutter. Approaching an SS officer, he asked if a doctor could not be found to treat the man. The officer started to bellow at Natalis, and he was immediately surrounded by a bunch of heavily-armed troopers. He felt the cold touch of steel on the back of his neck. Someone had jammed a pistol against his head. A voice said something in German and the pistol was removed. Peiper himself then appeared and Natalis appealed to him for someone to treat the children. If he could get a doctor, he thought, he would be able to convince him to help the wounded American; but his request was refused. Peiper shook his head firmly. 'All you people here in this region are terrorists,' he said.

Nevertheless Natalis felt he could win Peiper over. In his best classroom manner he asked him, 'Do you know the nature of the population around this region?' There was something of the teacher trying to catch out a small boy in the way he put the question. Peiper looked at him, but said nothing. Natalis then pulled out a small pocket diary for 1944. He turned the pages, until he found the page for January 21st, and showed it to Peiper. On it was drawn a simple diagram of an aeroplane. 'I made this mark,' he said, 'as a reminder. For on that day a German plane from Bremen destined for Chièvres, crashed a few kilometres north of Stoumont. Thirty-five German soldiers were on board. All the people from Stoumont turned out; the plane was on fire but we rescued as many as we could and took them to the hospital at Spa': He paused for a moment and then said, 'Our people are humanitarians, not terrorists.'

Peiper hesitated, then bowed slightly. Turning, he ordered the young officer to see that the people of Stoumont were not harmed.

Now Peiper had to get on. His men had done a good job of work that morning. If he could capture Targnon, a small town about a mile to the west where the Lienne flows into the Amblève, he could then turn south-west on a relatively good road along the west bank of the Lienne and take Chevron. There he would finally be able to break out of the Amblève valley.

But first he must force the Americans out of Stoumont railway station which was separated from the village by two kilometres of steep curving road. But even as he got ready to continue the attack, a sudden doubt clouded his mind. As he was to say later: 'We began to realise that we had insufficient gasoline to cross the bridge west of Stoumont.'

If Peiper was plagued with doubts as to the success of his next mission, the Americans preparing to oppose him were even more insecure. At his CP in Stoumont Station Colonel Sutherland of the 119th Infantry Regiment of the 30th Division knew that all that lay between his CP and Liège were the ten worn Shermans which had retreated from Stoumont. With a handful of shells left in their gun racks and manned by ordnance mechanics, this force was supposed to stand up to a whole German armoured battle group! Sutherland turned to General Hobbs, the divisional commander, who had come up to see for himself and explained the situation. Immediately, Hobbs contacted First Army HQ and told them the position, pointing out that there was supposed to be a new outfit, just arrived on the Continent, preparing to draw its tanks at the ordnance depot near Sprimont, about ten miles north of the 119th's CP. Could he have those tanks? He could. Hobbs turned and smiled at the worried regimental commander. The tanks were coming.

4

Back in Paris the daily evening briefing of the several score correspondents accredited to SHAEF headquarters had developed into an angry brawl. The newspapermen, who had been waiting for nearly three days for something concrete about the German breakthrough in the Ardennes, had had enough. They wanted facts and they wanted them now. Major James

Hughes, the briefing officer, tried to calm them, explaining that the news blackout had been imposed to prevent leaks to the enemy. The phrasing of his answer did not appease the correspondents' anger. 'Why don't you step down and let us hit at General Allen?' someone shouted. 'It's his place to answer these questions.'

Brigadier-General Allen, SHAEF Public Relations Head, rose to the bait. 'We're withholding news,' he said, 'to prevent the enemy from knowing the whereabouts of his own forward elements.' (He meant primarily Peiper, who, because of the poor quality of his communications equipment, was cut off from the rest of his division.)

George Lyons, SHAEF representative of the Office of War Information, lost his temper at what he thought was a stupid reply: 'May I say that SHAEF's policy on this matter is stupid!' he cried. 'And that's no reflection on you, sir. Everyone across hell and forty acres knows what's going on. The American people are entitled to know what's going on.' General Allen did not reply and the meeting broke up inconclusively.

The mood in the briefing room was typical of Allied headquarters that evening. The day, which had started in relative calmness, was threatening to turn into a nightmare. Everywhere the Germans were advancing. Nothing seemed able to stop them and there were alarming reports coming in of the conduct of some of the American units taking part in the fighting.

Alone in his room in the villa, the Supreme Commander was also seriously concerned. The Verdun Conference, which a few hours before had seemed to solve everything, now appeared to have solved nothing. Since he had returned, General Strong, his Intelligence Officer, had brought him more details of the German advance westwards. St Vith and Wiltz were about to fall. Bastogne probably wouldn't survive the night. Hourly the line of communication between Bradley's HQ in Luxemburg and Hodges' in Belgium was getting worse. It might soon be cut off altogether. What was Hodges to do then, cut off from his army group commander? Moreover his own communications with

Hodges at his new HQ at Chaudfontaine were bad because of his disrupted communications. Now, according to Strong, the German drive, led by Peiper, was being directed to Namur and northward. Under these circumstances, how could Bradley, who was determined not to leave Luxemburg City, give the northern shoulder of the Bulge the individual supervision it needed?

On that evening Eisenhower was faced with the most momentous decision of his career. The decisions he had taken a few short hours ago were no longer practical. What was he to do now?

General Strong had arrived back at headquarters at eight. The situation in the Ardennes was growing more serious by the hour. Not only were the Germans reinforcing their attack, but the now-identified 1 SS Panzer was getting ever closer to the 1st Army's huge supply dumps. Although they hadn't reached them yet, the Germans had somewhere or other obtained more fuel than intelligence had predicted they would be able to before the offensive. Now it appeared the enemy would be capable of continuing the attack for a longer period than had been anticipated, even if they did not capture the fuel dumps. Thus, as the reports came flooding in, one worse than the next, General Strong, like Eisenhower, began to wonder if the decisions made that day at Verdun had been sufficient.

German units were reported west of Bastogne heading for the Meuse. Something had been overlooked at the Verdun conference—the question of the overall command of the north in the threatened area of the Meuse had not been discussed. Now that question seemed to be of the utmost importance.

Finally Strong made up his mind. He took General Whiteley, acting head of the Operations Section and the other senior British officer at SHAEF, along to the Chief-of-Staff's quarters. Together they knocked the irritable General Bedell Smith out of bed.

The man who prided himself on being 'the son-of-a-bitch around this headquarters' was not particularly pleased to see them. His ulcer was acting up again and he did not like to lose what little sleep he could allow himself. Grumpily he asked the two British officers what they wanted. Quickly Strong related his misgivings, emphasising the fact that if Peiper or any of the other fast-moving German panzer columns reached the Meuse, they would succeed in driving a wedge right through the centre of General Bradley's command—and that meant his Army Group would be divided into two, with the northern sector no longer under his control.

Bedell Smith waited for Strong to finish his brief exposition and then asked him what he had to suggest. Strong cleared his throat. 'Montgomery seems to be the obvious choice to take the sector over,' he said as casually as he could.

5

Captain Berry of the 740th Tank Battalion was not at all happy with his first command in Europe. As the Shermans pulled out of the Sprimont Ordnance Depot behind him, he looked at them in disgust. They weren't what he expected to be taking into action with him for the first time. They were retreads: old battle-weary vehicles, patched up quickly at the Depot ready for some other brief action which would put an end to their combat career for good. They also had British radios which his crews did not know how to work. In action, therefore, he would have to rely on hand signals to give instructions, which he guessed, in spite of his lack of combat experience, wasn't too healthy for a commander if he had to poke his head out of the turret to do so.

But Berry had his orders. He was to take his company to a station near Stoumont and place himself at the disposal of the infantry regiment there, which was apparently in trouble.

The fog got progressively worse as he approached his destination. Standing in the turret of the lead tank, he could hear the crackle of small arms fire and the occasional harsh crack of a tank cannon. Anxiously he looked back at the company. They were keeping up, holding the regulation distance between vehicles as far as he could see. He gave the hand signal to slow down. They were getting near the scene of the fighting now. Suddenly, a hundred yards to his front, a cluster of buildings on the right-hand side of the road loomed up out of the fog. Then he saw the railway track and the signal and realised that this must be the station. Men of the shattered 3rd Battalion were everywhere, talking and gestulating excitedly. Many were helmetless and a few without weapons. Here and there a man squatted on the side of the road in the fog, hands dangling dejectly between his knees, staring straight ahead at nothing.

Just as Berry was debating where he should stop, another group of Shermans loomed up out of the fog on the opposite side of the road. They came on fast, their decks littered with infantrymen who looked as if they had just come out of action.

'We're low on ammo and fuel,' someone shouted across from the other group of tanks as they swept past.

'*And guts!*' Berry muttered to himself in disgust and decided to continue to the scene of the action, even if he had to go it completely alone with his company of beat-up tanks.

At dusk he got his orders from Colonel Herlong, C.O. of the 1st Battalion. He was to push ahead along the road to Stoumont, with Company C of the 1st Battalion of the 119th Infantry Regiment spread out to his right and left in the woods to prevent German infantry armed with *panzerfausts*, the German bazooka, from knocking the tanks out. The mixed infantry–tank group had as its objective the feeling-out of the enemy strength and the selecting of a suitable point of departure for a counter-attack on the village itself.

Berry gave the order to move out. The road in front of him was deserted. Everywhere there were the bits and pieces of equipment discarded by the 30th Division in their retreat, but that was all. He turned in his turret and gave Lieutenant Powers to his rear a hand signal to advance and take up the point with his platoon of five tanks. Powers acknowledged and while Berry's tank drew to one side, the platoon rattled by.

Abruptly a Panther loomed up out of the fog immediately to Powers' front. For one moment neither tank reacted. Then Powers' gunner's 75 mm roared into life. There was the echoing sound of metal striking metal. A spurt of flame erupted along the Panther's gun mantlet and the white-hot armour-piercing shell ricochetted down, killing the driver and gunner immediately. Powers rumbled on past the stricken enemy tank, elated at his first kill.

Now the fog and the drizzle which had begun to fall, plus the growing darkness, made it virtually impossible to see more than twenty yards ahead. Up ahead barring the road a huge tank loomed out of the fog. Again Powers reacted first. His gunner fired almost immediately. The shell glanced harmlessly off the steeply-inclined plate of the Tiger's front.

Powers bellowed at his gunner to fire again. But the newly-installed gun jammed. Frantically the gunner tried to repair the fault. The Tiger started to move in, bringing its huge gun to bear on the Sherman. In desperation Powers stood up in the turret, and signalled to the rear for help.

It came in the form of a 90 mm tank-destroyer, which Berry had also brought along from the ordnance depot. But before it could get into a position to fire, the Tiger fired. The first shot missed, and the second. By then the TD was in position. It fired and the Tiger went up in flames.

'It's clear,' Powers' gunner shouted above the din. Powers rattled forward. To his right the Tiger was burning fiercely, the flames mixed with a mass of thick oily smoke. The Sherman thrust through the smoke. Before it was another Panther. Again Powers fired first. The shot struck the cobbles, flew up off the road and penetrated the tank's flooring. Desperately the German tried to retreat. The American gunner fired once again and hit the Panther's muzzle-brake. The end of the German gun flew high into the air. The tank came to an abrupt halt and burst into flames.

The German attack was over. In thirty minutes Captain Berry's scratch force had stopped the retreat and so impressed the German armoured point and its commander that he ordered the remaining vehicles to withdraw up the hill to the cover of the Stoumont defences. Peiper, when he learned what had happened, concurred. His fuel was almost gone. He couldn't afford to waste what precious little he had left in a protracted tank battle.

Encouraged by Berry's success, the infantrymen of the 119th Infantry began to plod once more up the hill down which they had so recently retreated. Before them Peiper's outposts started to withdraw. The 1 SS were stalled again.

Behind the immediate front in the Amblève area, a new force started to make itself felt. Airborne Corps Commander General Ridgway had arrived to co-ordinate the defence. Setting up his headquarters just behind that of General Gavin of the 82nd Airborne at Werbomont, he had a hard look at the situation and the forces at his disposal. His mission was to block any further advance by Peiper along an irregular line from the Amblève down to the River Ourthe, where his XVIII Airborne Corps was threatened by other elements of the German offensive. In addition, he had the task of sealing the twenty mile gap which had been opened between V and VIII Corps by the 6th SS Panzer Army's advance.

The forces at his disposal were a mixed lot. He had the 30th Division's 119th Infantry Regiment, Gavin's 82nd Airborne and, coming from the north, a combat command of the 3rd Armored Division. These were the units he would use to defeat Peiper. The 82nd would push a 'defensive screen' forward in what was really an offensive role north, east, south and west of Werbomont. The combat command from the Third, would, when it arrived, link up with the 117th Infantry and with its help secure the Amblève River line from Stoumont to La Gleize. In the meantime part of the 82nd would take over the defense of the Salm River bridges at Trois Ponts, drive the enemy from the area between the River Amblève and the Werbomont–Trois Ponts road, and make contact with the 3rd Armored Combat

Command when the latter reached Stavelot, thus completing the encirclement of all enemy forces left to the north.

While General Ridgway completed his plans for the morrow, Colonel Peiper also took stock of his situation. It was not good. Far to his rear the 6th SS Panzer Army had still not succeeded in broadening its area of breakthrough sufficiently for the second wave of armour to push ahead and give him the vitally-needed support he required to swamp the American opposition. His supplies, especially of fuel, were running low, and the American action at Stavelot having cut off his major supply route, meant that he would have to rely on air supply until Stavelot could be recaptured.

At present he was limited to an area of a few square kilometres, centred on La Gleize and Stoumont with an outpost holding a light bridge across the Amblève at Cheneux. In this tight little position, he had his 1st Battalion of the 1st Panzer Regiment defending Stoumont, his 2nd Battalion of the same regiment doing the same in La Gleize. At Cheneux, he had the 84th Light Flak Battalion, supported by the 2nd Grenadier Regiment. His men were still in good heart and they had only suffered light casualties during their assault on Stoumont that morning, but the spirit of the day before had vanished. He suspected that his men realised that the attack of *Kampfgruppe* Peiper had been stalled for good. The drive west had come to an end. Now it was going to be a fight for survival.

And down below just at a turn of the bend that led to Stoumont Railway Station the Panther knocked out by Captain Berry's company still smouldered in the darkness, while all around the sounds of battle died away. It was midnight on the 19th of December. The wrecked Panther marked the furthest penetration westwards Jochen Peiper would ever make.

Day Five:

WEDNESDAY, 20 DECEMBER, 1944

'Like Christ come to cleanse the temple'
British officer describing Field-Marshal
Montgomery's entry to General Hodges' Headquarters.

The NCOs crept stealthily from man to man where they lay sprawled in the rubble of the shattered houses that lined the river at Stavelot. 'Wake up!' they hissed, 'They're coming!' Suddenly there was the sound of metal striking metal. Almost immediately a red flare soared into the sky and hung momentarily over the river, bathing it in a ruddy light. There they were— a line of Germans spread out in the shallows on the other side, wading through the water, rifles held high above their heads.

A ragged crackle of rifles erupted from the line of houses held by the Americans. A machine-gun began to chatter, sending a stream of white and green tracer dots and dashes across the water. Then the flare fell into the water and darkness returned. From the other side of the river machine-guns opened up. Slow streams of white tracer came from half-a-dozen widely separated positions.

Frantically the young officer in charge of the platoon in the path of the German attack rattled the field telephone and cried for more flares. As they lit up the scene there was time for a brief glimpse of scores of Germans struggling through the water.

Lieutenant Jean Hansen, commanding a section of the 743rd Tank Battalion, which was supporting the infantry, made a quick decision. 'Load incendiary!' he ordered. Swiftly his gunners withdrew the armour-piercing shells and replaced them with incendiaries. 'Fire!' Hansen roared. All along the small row of houses on the German side of the river, the shells struck home, exploding in clouds of white smoke. Swiftly the flames rose as the houses began to burn. And as the light silhouetted the men in the water the GIs turned their fire on them once more.

Sergeant William Pierce had the same idea as the young tank officer. Grabbing a couple of jerricans full of gasoline, he waded into the river and managed to struggle across undetected. Staggering to the nearest house he sloshed the gasoline over its front and set light to it. It went up in a whoosh of red and yellow flame. Then he fled back the way he had come.

The 'duck shoot', as the GIs were to call it afterwards, began. It was a wild unforgettable scene of murder and mayhem. The Germans, their silhouettes clear against the ever-mounting flames on the other bank, were helplessly trapped. Dead and dying fell into the water; as screams and cries for help rang out. But still they came on, 'like men drugged,' Lieutenant Murray, commanding 1st Platoon, remembered years later.

In the houses the GIs began to enjoy the killing. Their fear had vanished now, as well as their exhaustion. An abrupt, almost atavistic, lust to kill overcame them. Their first hectic firing had been replaced by a careful deliberate selection of the best victims. A young officer, recognisable by the cap he wore instead of the helmet of the others, turned his head to wave on his men. A sight focussed on him and he fell dead the next instant, a bullet through his chest. A big man with a machine-pistol held high above his head, waded through the river. The black metal sight cut his face in half, the soft squeeze on the round trigger, the hard thump against the aimer's shoulder and the man staggered back, his face a mass of blood. One by one they fell until at last there were no more of them there and the river carried their corpses away under the bridge.

But Colonel Sandig of the *Leibstandarte* was not a man to give up in a hurry, in spite of the fact that the first attempted crossing had cost him over forty dead. Now he ordered direct tank fire to be brought on the American positions nearest the river. Immediately the Tigers cracked into action, bringing their guns to bear at almost point-blank range.

The triumphant mood of the Americans vanished at once. Bricks and mortar tumbled down all about them. The night was hideous with the roar of the enemy guns. Huge red-hot fragments of steel flew through the air. Under the cover of the barrage the German infantry crossed the river.They ran from house to house, firing a quick burst, hesitating, firing and then running on again. Lieutenant Murray's 1st Platoon, unable to hold, was forced back. They abandoned the first row of houses, giving and taking casualties. They scrambled into the next row. Here Murray knew that he was out of range of direct German fire. His men could rest for the moment.

Then, summoning up help from Company B, Murray ordered his survivors out into the street again. The Germans had not yet dug in in the first row of houses; it was a surprising oversight. They usually dug in in any newly captured position immediately. Desperately they tried to hold the Americans back as they were driven down to the edge of the river. The Americans pressed on relentlessly.

Now the first light of dawn began to reveal the brutal reality of man's inhumanity to man. The dead were everywhere, among the ruined houses and on the edge of the river, where the surviving Germans were now breaking and running back through the fast-flowing water. On the far bank the houses were still burning. At the middle tier of the bridge a couple of dead bodies had been halted in their passage downstream and were bumping back and forth with the current.

By 7.30 the American line on the south side of the Amblève had been re-established and Stavelot was firmly in American hands, not to be lost again. At last the defenders were able to relax.

General William Harrison, assistant divisional commander of the 30th Infantry Division, was angry. Unlike General Hobbs,

his superior, he hated to be tied to a desk in a divisional headquarters; he liked to be up front with the men, and although he
was a strict disciplinarian, his liking for the front line had won
him the nickname 'the GIs' General' in the 30th Division.

But yesterday he had witnessed something he had never
anticipated he would see in the 30th Division—the flight of
Sutherland's 3rd Battalion down the hill from Stoumont. He
had immediately recommended the regimental commander's
relief and suggested he take over the command. Hobbs had
agreed. Now he found himself suddenly detached from the
Division and under the command of the XVIII Airborne Corps,
and he knew that General Ridgway was a soldier who did not
understand the meaning of failure. Together with General
Truman Boudinot's Combat Command B of the 3rd Armored
Division moving down from the north, he had been ordered to
put the squeeze on the Stoumont area, his job being the capture
of the key village itself. And the 119th United States Infantry
were not going to fail again!

But if the new commander of the 119th Infantry, now renamed
Task Force Harrison, expected his revitalised command to fight
its way up the hill into Stoumont with the dash of the cavalry
from which he came, he was mistaken. Led by Berry's tank
company from the 740th Tank Battalion, the infantry advanced
cautiously, fighting their way through minefields covered by
enemy snipers and anti-tank guns which made them pay for
every yard of ground they covered. Berry's command suffered too
from German tanks dug in on the surrounding hillside. Yet in
spite of the opposition, Colonel Herlong, well aware of what had
happened to his regimental commander the day before and of
General Harrison's temper, did not flag. Time and time again he
urged his men on to new efforts whenever they appeared to be
weakening so that if their progress was not spectacular it was at
least steady.

The attacking force covered the first thousand yards. A
minefield barred the way and had to be covered by an infantry
force flanking it on the wooded hillside to the left of the road

while engineers cleared a path for the tanks. Another thousand yards, and another minefield which cost Berry two of his precious Shermans. Yard by yard they crawled forward. Now the St Edouard's Sanatorium, the largest building in Stoumont, loomed up to their left. It looked from below like a fortress guarding the road. Two company commanders decided spontaneously it would make good CPs for them and sent small bodies of infantry to take it. The infantry hurried off while the advance continued. The third thousand yards was almost achieved.

Up in St Edouard's Sanitorium the Germans waited for the advancing Americans. Their position gave them a commanding view of the road below. Indeed, the SS men had boasted to the two hundred sick children and old people in the cellars below them that this was their *'Festung Sankt Eduard* (Fortress St Edward). But the overconfident SS men had not reckoned with the fog which was beginning to roll in from the surrounding hills.

The artillery bombardment was their first warning that the Americans were upon them. It was sharp, short and effective. It kept their heads down, away from the tall, shattered windows. When it ceased the khaki-clad figures of the *Amis* were slipping through the grounds and into the first out-buildings.

A brisk fire-fight broke out, its sound muted by the fog. But there were too many of the *Amis* and too few of the SS. The Americans started to push them back. Soon they were in the main building itself and the corridors echoed to the chatter of machine-guns, the heavy thud of bodies thrown violently to the floor and the crash as bazooka shells penetrated the inner walls.

Down below in the great candle-lit cellar, two priests and several nuns wearing huge starched winged caps and dressed in blue habits tried to calm the old people and the terrified tubercular children. Father Hanlet, the senior priest, made them kneel and clasp their hands together, and above the roar of the battle, shouting in a way he had never shouted before, he led them in prayer.

The mumble of the prayer rose and fell, then broke off

altogether. Above them the shooting had stopped. Silence reigned. Father Hanlet raised himself from his knees stiffly, and turned to the door of the cellar expectantly.

Then it swung open. There was a burst of machine pistol fire in the stairwell. 'Civilians!' the people in the cellar cried panic-stricken. 'We're civilians!' A man in khaki, rifle in hand, appeared through the door. It was an American! 'Sammy! . . . Sammy!' the children shouted joyfully, running towards him.

Others followed him through the door to be surrounded by the overexcited children, their yellow faces flushed with the hectic red spots of the tubercular. Hurriedly the 'white swans', as the children called the nuns, rushed forward to calm them. Making them kneel, the Mother Superior started to recite the rosary, then asked for eternal peace for those who had fallen in the battle which had taken place above their heads.

Down below Colonel Herlong judged that it was time to call a halt. That day his command had covered 3,000 yards. It was not a spectacular advance, but it had made up in part for yesterday's retreat. Fog was beginning to become a problem as well and he felt it was time to secure his positions before the fog became too thick. He ordered his men to close in for the night. One of the two tanks disabled in the minefield was turned sideways to block the road. Between this roadblock and the sanatorium he placed four of Berry's tanks, then ordered his B and C companies to dig in in a semi-circle on the hillside around the sanatorium itself. Quickly a defensive position was established, while only 300 yards away the enemy foxhole line lay still and mysterious, without any apparent movement. Then the fog descended totally obscuring sight and deadening sound.

2

While the American infantrymen at Stavelot were crushing Colonel Sandig's SS men, General Strong, in his office at

Versailles, was getting his things ready for departure. It was a sad moment for him. He had been with the Supreme Commander for nearly two years. The American débâcle at Kasserine had brought him to Eisenhower's headquarters to help sort out the mess. Now another mess, the Ardennes, seemed to have sealed his fate. It was obvious that Bedell Smith had lost confidence in him and in Whiteley because of their suggestion of the night before. This morning Bedell Smith would undoubtedly recommend to Eisenhower that he and Whiteley should go.

It was time to go to the morning briefing. Strong took a last look at the room which had been his office for the last two months and walked down the corridor to the conference room. Before him Whiteley walked alone. Normally he went in with Bedell Smith, but this morning, still angry at Smith's outburst of the previous evening, he made a point of entering the room by himself.

The conference got down to business, Bedell Smith who was presiding, limiting himself to glum grunts and bad-tempered interruptions. Then when it was finished, he suddenly walked over to General Strong and took him by the arm. Quietly and without any apparent sign of emotion, he told him that he was going to recommend to Eisenhower that he accept Montgomery as commander of the northern sector of the front. Strong was staggered. This was an astonishing turn-round on Smith's part but he did not seem to notice his colleague's surprise and continued as calmly as before, telling Strong that he must keep his mouth shut when they went to see Eisenhower. The proposal must appear to come from Smith. It would look better from an American than from a Britisher. Strong nodded his agreement.

A little later they entered the Supreme Commander's office and General Whiteley began the briefing. But he had hardly started when Eisenhower interrupted him: 'Jock, I think you had an idea last night to give the northern half of this battlefield to Monty. What about that?'

Whiteley hesitated, and Smith broke in. 'Yes sir, that is so.'

Eisenhower picked up the 'phone and asked for General

Bradley. It was a long conversation and a heated one. Although they only heard one side of it the three men knew from the look on the Supreme Commander's face and from the tone of his voice that General Bradley was opposing the Montgomery appointment. Finally Eisenhower said softly but firmly, 'Well, Brad, those are my orders,' and put down the 'phone.

The die was cast. Field-Marshal Sir Bernard Montgomery was to take over command of the 1st Army and with that, as he already had one American army, the Ninth, under his command, he would be in command of more American troops than General Bradley himself. Far away in Stoumont Colonel Peiper did not realise that his armoured thrust had led to an appointment that was to create a greater and longer-lasting rift between the British and Americans than any other offensive of the war. On 20 December the foundation of *the* major breakdown in the relations between the Allies was laid.

At Chaudfontaine General Hodges was waiting for his new chief with mixed feelings. He knew Montgomery's reputation and what to expect when he took over, but at the same time he was glad not to have to face the awful burden of alone making the decisions upon which the future of his whole army might depend. In truth, General Hodges was tired. None of the other four armies under Bradley's command had borne such a strain as had his that winter. From the end of October onwards he had been forced to fight on the most important sector of the front against the strongest portion of the enemy's force in the most rugged of terrain. In the Hürtgen Forest and the Roer he had fought as best he could, under-manned, under-supplied with General Patton's Third Army undeniably receiving much stronger support from General Bradley. Now he was faced with the greatest crisis of all—two grave gaps torn in his front, and no advice or control from his army group commander. He would be glad to have some advice from a man like Montgomery, who, whatever his failings may be, was a thorough, highly experienced commander.

Montgomery arrived at noon, together with his acting Chief-of-Staff, Brigadier Belchem. He was dressed in a hip-length jacket and baggy khaki trousers with a thick scarf wrapped round his neck. Instead of the traditional black beret, he wore a red paratrooper's beret adorned with the twin badges. He had just been appointed colonel-commandant of the Parachute Regiment and with his usual flair for publicity, had decided that his new headgear would undoubtedly attract attention from the journalists.

For weeks Montgomery had been feeling that the war was passing him by; his attempts to convince Eisenhower to concentrate a major section of the Allied forces under his command for one final attack on the enemy had been ignored. Ever since the failure of his Arnhem landing, which was the boldest and most un-Montgomery-like operation he had ever planned, he had felt like a prophet in the wilderness. Now he had been given command of a great American army and virtual carte blanche to handle it any way he liked. His spirits soared; he was going into action again under his own terms.[1]

Briskly he stepped out of his Humber, and strode into the US Headquarters. His sharp birdlike face was alert, cheerful and supremely self-assured so that a young British officer, watching the fateful entrance from the sidelines, was later to confess that he had the appearance of 'Christ come to cleanse the temple'. He was ushered into the conference room, where he paused and stared round the half-circle of American staff officers. 'Well, gentlemen,' he said in his upper-class British voice, 'I gather that a difficult situation had arisen. Now *do* tell me the form'. After he had been briefed, he sent for his picnic basket and sat thoughtfully munching his sandwiches, mulling over the

[1] There is still considerable doubt about *who* exactly made the suggestion to Strong and Whiteley to have Montgomery appointed commander of the northern section of the US defence in the Ardennes. There is some evidence to show that the original suggestion *might* have come from Montgomery's own HQ on the evening of 19 Dec. However, it is clear that for obvious reasons of national and personal prestige, those still alive who are in a position to know will not reveal the real background to this key appointment that changed the whole course of the battle.

information he had just been given. Then he excused himself and went to another room where his 'eyes and ears' were waiting for him. These six young officers, not one of them higher in rank than a major, had been out visiting the various sectors of the front, patiently questioning commanders and using their battle-trained eyes to assess the situation. They gave their chief their frank assessments of the 1st Army front.

A little later he returned to the waiting 1st Army staff officers in the conference room and began to give out his orders. Unlike Hodges, who thought Liège was the main objective on the Meuse, Montgomery felt the section of the river south of the town was the German target (Intelligence had told him the Luftwaffe had orders *not* to bomb the bridges in that area). Accordingly he felt that reserves should be assembled to counter-attack at some later date and in order to find these men, the 1st Army line should be shortened; in other words a withdrawal.

Hodges almost took the suggestion as a personal insult. He was adamant. 'No,' he said firmly, 'American troops will not withdraw'.

The discussion might have gone on a long time if at that moment an exhausted officer wearing the divisional patch of the 7th Armored Division had not appeared. He was Colonel Fred Schroeder who had just made his way out of embattled St Vith where his division was virtually surrounded and being attacked by three enemy divisions.

With a mumbled introduction, he handed a note written in pencil by his divisional commander, General Hasbrouck, to Hodges' Chief-of-Staff, General Kean. The latter read it and passed it to Hodges, saying: 'Gentlemen, I think you'll find this news from St Vith interesting.' It was. After detailing the critical situation of his command, Hasbrouck ended with restrained words which, because they were so restrained, revealed the seriousness of his position: 'VII Corps has ordered me to hold and I will do so, but need help. An attack from Bastogne to the north-east will relieve the situation and in turn cut the bastards off in the rear. I also need plenty of air support ... Understand

82nd Airborne Division is coming up on my north and the north flank is not critical.'

Hodges waited a moment to let the full impact of the letter sink in, then cleared his throat. The dramatic appeal for help had hardened his attitude to withdrawal: 'In the light of this new information,' he said, 'Ridgway's Eighteenth Corps will have to keep driving forward to St Vith to Hasbrouck's relief.'

For the time being the Field-Marshal gave in and allowed the letter to dictate immediate policy. 'I agree that the chaps in St Vith must be helped,' he said, but went on to state that the operation had to be carried out *his* way. Ridgway was to 're-establish the line Malmédy–St Vith' and thus regain contact with the 7th Armored in St Vith. Peiper's force, which was the major impediment in the way of the 82nd Airborne and Combat Command B of the 3rd Armored, the two units which were going to make the link-up, had to be eradicated *at once*. But once the link-up had been established, St Vith would be evacuated, for as Montgomery said, getting to his feet to go, 'You can't win a big victory without a tidy show, can you?' And then he was gone.

3

That afternoon the two units Montgomery had scheduled to link up with the 7th Armored in St Vith—General Boudinot's Combat Command B of the 3rd Armored and General Gavin's 82nd Airborne—were already in action against Peiper's force, which they would have to defeat if they were to carry out their recue action.

Boudinot had hit the Germans first. Dividing his force into three, Task Force Lovelady, Task Force McGeorge and Task Force Jordan (all named after their commanders), he was now pushing them down three separate roads from the north in the general direction of Stoumont–La Gleize. Task Force Lovelady, the biggest outfit, which formed the left jaw of a vice made of armour about to clamp down on *Kampfgruppe* Peiper, reached the junction of the Trois Ponts–Stoumont roads without seeing a sign of the enemy. In fact the whole area seemed deserted, as if the rumour of the coming of the SS had caused a mass flight of the civilian population.

Colonel Bill Lovelady, commander of the force, surveyed the scene. It looked peaceful enough to him. Then he made up his mind. The column rolled on. But they hadn't gone more than a couple of hundred yards when they ran into the enemy. Turning round a bend in the road that ran to Trois Ponts, a small German convoy, its vehicles laden with branches hastily ripped from the woods and entwined in camouflaged nets, was rolling directly towards them. The Germans were as surprised as the 3rd Armored tankers. They were a small supply train which had passed over a reinforced bridge that had been discovered east of Trois Ponts. Now they were trying to sneak in the much-needed gasoline to the almost surrounded Peiper.

It was the Americans who overcame their surprise first. The 75 mm of the lead Sherman cracked into action. The closest German truck went up in flames. Other Shermans joined in the kill. More trucks were hit and began to burn fiercely. Hurriedly the Germans abandoned their vehicles and flung themselves in the ditches on both sides of the narrow road. Within minutes it was all over and the beaten SS men were coming out of their hiding places, hands above their heads, advancing past their burning vehicles towards the suspicious Americans.

Lovelady ordered the advance to continue. His forty-five Shermans rolled smoothly down the road towards Trois Ponts. There they scattered a handful of SS men from Knittel's group holed up in the house of M. Habotte and rescued a handful of terrified Belgian civilians who had been expecting to be shot at any moment. They contacted Major Yates' engineers who were still defending their bank of the river against the constant efforts of German reconnaissance patrols to penetrate their lines. Although they now numbered less than a hundred men, they had fooled the experienced SS commanders for three days by such devices as simulating armoured reinforcements by putting chains on a four-ton truck and running it up and down the village street during the night, or taking bazookas into the woods and firing them as if they were distant artillery. For a little while the two groups exchanged experiences, then Lovelady pushed on once more in the direction of Stavelot.

But now their luck deserted them. Just as they were approaching the hamlet of Petit-Spai, the point ran into a trap. In a group of houses to the right of the road the Germans had dug in half-a-dozen light anti-tank guns, supporting them with three heavy tanks, hull down, on both sides of the Amblève. The six unsuspecting tanks rumbled on along the deserted road. Just as they reached the crossroads in the centre of the hamlet, the German tanks and anti-tank guns opened up.

Every one of the six Shermans was hit immediately. In rapid succession each tank went up in flames, ignited by the explosion close to their highly sensitive gasoline engines, which had earned for them the truthful but unpleasant nickname of 'Ronson lighters'. Hurriedly the crews baled out and scrambled for cover, followed by German machine-gun fire. The advance of Task Force Lovelady had come to an end. With the road completely blocked by a determined enemy and by the glowing Shermans, Lovelady ordered his force to pull back. Hastily, and with many a curse at the tightness of the road which did not allow them to turn, the drivers reversed the way they had come.

The two remaining task forces had little better luck that day. Major McGeorge's group, approaching La Gleize from the north-east, had an easy start. It advanced along a high ridge road to within two miles of La Gleize without sight of the enemy. However, just as it left the village of Cour, where McGeorge had picked up a company of infantry, the force ran slap into a German roadblock. Hastily the infantry sprang from the decks of the tanks and deployed against it. A sharp counter-attack drove them back, and when the German infantry began to approach ever closer to his tanks, Major McGeorge decided that it was time he pulled back. Hurriedly he retired to the hamlet of Borgoumont.

Task Force Jordan, under Captain John Jordan, fared little better. This, the smallest of the three task forces, had approached to within sight of Stoumont, when they too were surprised by flanking fire from enemy tanks dug in on the hillside. Two Shermans were hit almost immediately and Jordan knew that if he didn't do something soon his little force would suffer heavy losses—they were perched on the road like sitting ducks. He could not deploy, on account of the thick forest on the other side of the road, so that all that was left to him was to withdraw. Swiftly he gave the necessary order and his Shermans began to pull back along the road until they were out of reach of the enemy tank fire.

If Peiper was trapped by lack of fuel, he was making it amply clear that he was not going to give up his gains easily. That the 3rd Armored had learned to their cost on the first day of combat against the *I SS Leibstandarte Adolf Hitler*.

So had the 82nd Airborne men engaged in closing the circle around Peiper by erasing the small German bridgehead at Cheneux on the Amblève south-east of Stoumont.

Ordered to get to Cheneux and capture the bridge as soon as possible, Colonel Reuben Tucker of the 504th Gliderborne Infantry sent two companies of his 1st Battalion to the village. About mid-afternoon the lead company reached the outskirts and immediately came under intense machine-gun fire, followed by light flak from multiple flak cannon. They scattered at once and returned the fire. It was clear from the volume of the fire and the red crackle of light from the huddle of buildings to the Americans' front, that Cheneux was strongly defended. The airborne officers decided to wait for further orders.

They were not long in coming. Gavin had just received orders to advance south-east and help in the relief of St Vith. He had no time to waste on this German bridgehead, which had to be rubbed out at once. He relayed his orders to Colonel Tucker, who told the C.O. of the 1st Battalion, Lieutenant-Colonel

Harrison to take the two companies already at Cheneux and launch a night attack. Harrison hurried to Cheneux and held a brief conference. The officers listened in silence and with growing anxiety as they realised what Harrison was asking of them. They were to attack a fortified village, with only two tank destroyers as heavy support. If that weren't enough, their approach to the village would bring them across a stretch of ground, completely barren of cover, criss-crossed with barbed wire and sloping gradually to the German positions, held by Sandig's 2nd Panzer Grenadier Regiment who were armed, as they had learned during the period of waiting, with mobile assault artillery.

There was nothing for it but to obey orders. Swiftly the officers dispersed to pass on their orders to the men crouched in hastily scooped holes in the ground. The men took the news as silently as their officers had, but their eyes flickered anxiously over the commanders' shoulders, staring at the village on the hill, waiting for them in silence. At 1930, the attacking force formed up astride the road west of Cheneux, with the TDs holding the road itself. Cautiously they began to advance through the soaked fields, the only sound that of their own heavy breathing and the occasional rattle of equipment, each man wrapped in his own mantle of fear for what this night would bring.

A lone machine-gun began to chatter; a slow line of white dots and dashes came towards them. Somewhere an officer shouted a command. The pace of the advance quickened. Blue flames shot out of the TDs' exhausts as they put on speed. Now they were coming to the stretch of bare ground that sloped up to the village. The fire from the village began to intensify. The infantry were half-doubling. The TD in the lead started to spray the approach to the village with tracer. Suddenly there was the first crack of the 20 mm flak cannon. They were at the stretch of bare ground.

The plan was to rush the four hundred yards of open terrain in four waves at intervals of fifty yards, hoping that the darkness might save them. The first wave was ready. So were the Germans. As they rushed forward, stumbling in the darkness, the enemy opened up with intense and accurate fire. The whole top of the hillside blazed in furious light and the line of red explosions ran frantically from house to house. Seconds later the hail of fire descended upon the Airborne men. Men dropped everywhere, screaming, cursing, groaning, clapping hands to ruined faces, shattered knees, holed chests. Great gaps appeared in the line. But they kept going for a minute . . . for two . . . three. Then they broke, fleeing from that terrible wall of fire, crashing through the next wave, bowling over their comrades in the darkness, one thought only in their minds—*flight*.

The second wave struggled bravely on. Then it was their turn. Up on the hillside the machine-guns chattered their message of death once more. The flak guns began to thump. Zig-zag lines of tracer raced towards them. Again huge gaps were torn in their line. Again the line broke and ran.

But help was on its way. The two TDs had worked their way up to the edge of the slope, and now they opened fire. For an instant, the infantry could see the armoured vehicles outlined in a flash of vivid light, then darkness. Slowly the 90 mm shells at close range began to have their effect and the volume of enemy fire slackened.

It was Company C's turn. They dashed boldly up the hill. This time, although they took heavy casualties, they made it. Suddenly there were curses and angry shouts everywhere. Here and there a man tripped and fell heavily in the darkness. They had run into a wired position! Helpless without wire cutters their attack faded away.

The TDs moved closer. Their fire rate intensified. Now it was time for the fourth assault. It went in, stumbling over the bodies of those already dead. But the TDs were having an effect. The rate of enemy fire was beginning to slacken. Men were falling but not so frequently as in the first waves. Their ranks were growing thinner, but they weren't breaking. Now the village houses loomed up in front of them. A German came running out.

A dozen men fired from the hip as they advanced. He fell heavily. Another appeared. An NCO with a machine pistol gave him a burst. He dropped without a sound. Then they were in among the houses. Crazy with anger at their commanders who had set them this impossible task, at the Germans who had killed so many of their comrades and at the world which allowed such things, they brooked no resistance. The German defenders were shot down mercilessly. Hurriedly they retreated to the second line of houses, firing as they went.

The attack was over. The surviving officers collected their men and made them dig in, setting up the best defence they could in this slight toehold in Cheneux until reinforcements arrived. Numbly, the survivors set about their task, while the slugs whacked unnoticed into the walls of the little houses around them.

4

Silence had descended over the sanatorium outside Stoumont. On the shattered first floor the weary GIs had settled down for the night among the rubble. Down below in the cellar the civilians also tried to sleep, consoled by the thought that Father Hanlet had promised they would be evacuated the following day; this was to be their last night of discomfort.

Just before midnight, the German counter-attack came. Crying and yelling they rushed down the hill, firing as they ran. In an instant everything was panic in the sanatorium. Down in the cellars the women tried to comfort the children; the old ones pressed their hands tightly across their breasts or bit the ends of their fingers to prevent themselves from crying out, while the nuns rushed from one end of the room to the other.

Up above on the pitch-black first floor everything was a confused mess of shouted order and counter-order. Men dashed back and forth in the littered darkness, crashing heavily to the ground every now and again. Inside the main corridor a machine-gun began to hammer. Immediately it attracted German counter-fire and slugs started slamming into the walls.

Cannon fire hit the Sanatorium at close range from above and rocked it with every hit scored. The German tanks, in unseen positions somewhere in the darkness just above the building, revealed their presence by the abrupt scarlet stream of flame that shot out into the night over and over again. Frantically, the officers shouted for help over the radio phone. Down below the section of Shermans positioned between the building and the roadblock revved their engines. They tried to take the hill, but the ground had not been surveyed and their tracks slipped as the drivers roared their engines to no avail. The slope was too steep.

Suddenly a soft crump sounded from below. It was followed a second later by a stream of angry red sparks. The veterans of the 30th Division knew what that meant. The Krauts were in among the tanks with their panzerfausts! There was the crash of metal against metal. A Sherman went up in a sheet of flame that leaped thirty feet in the air. A second later its ammunition began to explode, zig-zagging off in all directions. Another was hit, and another. A Tiger crept down the hill towards them, its long gun swinging from side to side. The Berry company began to back off. They were sitting ducks in the ruddy light of the fiercely burning Shermans.

Up above in the sanatorium, the infantry, sprawled in the rubble, knew it was their turn to get it now. The German tanks rumbled closer and closer. Crouched in their hastily occupied positions, the GIs still couldn't see them, but they could hear them, only a matter of yards away.

Then the first Tiger loomed up out of the darkness. When it fired, the whole building shook. Hurriedly the defenders backed away from the windows. German infantry made their appearance now, running between the tanks. A stick-grenade sailed through a shattered window in heavy slow motion. It exploded harmlessly. It was followed by another and another. The Americans retreated even further. Some dropped in the fresh piles of rubble and waited for the first Germans to clamber through the shattered line of windows they had just evacuated. Others cast away their rifles and threw themselves out of the rear windows onto the ground below.

A Tiger thrust its long-barrelled gun through a window, splintering the remaining glass. Horrified, the GIs crouched in a corner watching as the gun swung from side to side. It fired. Frantically they clapped their hands to their ears. The noise was horrific. Huge clouds of dust rose from the floor and plaster began to fall from the ceiling like snow. A German soldier poked his head cautiously above the window sill from outside just as the Tiger fired. Thus illuminated he made a perfect target. For the hidden GI it was like being on the range shooting at 'snap' targets. The German fell back, gurgling blood and clasping his throat. But there were more behind him. Steadily they clambered through the windows and drove the defenders from room to room. Finally there was nowhere to go and the surviving Americans emerged from their last hiding places, throwing away their weapons and raising their hands in defeat.

A few refused to surrender, however. Sergeant William Widener, with eleven men under his command, fought a fierce battle of his own in an outlying building to which he had retreated. Organising his men in some semblance of an all-round defence, he beat back all the Germans could throw at him, shouting ranging instructions all the time to an artillery observer crouched in a trench some fifty yards behind him, who passed them on to the artillery. Under his cover the survivors of the two shattered companies in the sanatorium hastily organised a fresh defence line to the rear of Sergeant Widener, who was later to receive a decoration for his bravery on that wild December night.

This time the defenders of the new line, which was a mud-filled ditch, did not relax. Just before dawn the Germans came again. The Americans were waiting, reinforced by Berry's tanks. The combined fire of the two forces broke the German attack almost before it had started. It withered away under the volume of American fire. When dawn broke the field in front of the American position was like a lunar landscape, pitted with craters and littered with the ugly forms of the dead. This time the Americans had held firm, but Peiper had captured St Edward's Sanatorium, the key to Stoumont.

During the night of 20/21 December Companies B and C of the 1st Battalion of the 119th Infantry Regiment had lost half their effective strength, including five platoon leaders. Down in the cellars of the sanatorium, the Germans were sorting out the thirty-two Americans they had taken prisoner.

Hands over their heads, some wounded, some shocked, they stared at their captors, who were searching them. A big SS man with a week's growth of beard, who appeared to be the leader, took out one GI's identity card and after looking at it, waved it over his head, crying: 'Look at this! Even a *Herr Leutnant!*' The tired young Second Lieutenant blushed like a schoolboy.

Finished with the search, the SS marched them away to the bakery, while in the cellar a wounded man was left behind to the ministrations of a nun who was trying to apply a tourniquet to his badly shattered right arm. Father Henlet, kneeling at her side, knew the man was going to die: he began to administer the last rites. Suddenly the dying man's eyes flickered open and he looked at the priest's gentle face. 'Thanks,' he said in English, 'I'm not a catholic. But my wife is. She'll be happy—in case I die.' The bearded German NCO who had laughed at the boyish American lieutenant was moved. He put a coarse black tobacco German cigarette between the wounded man's lips and lit it. The American puffed a little, coughed and then fumbling in his jacket pocket with his good hand, brought out a small piece of ration chocolate.

Carefully he handed it to the priest and said: 'For the German comrade'. The German took it with an attempt at a bow and smiled at the dying man. Then he turned and whispered to Father Hanlet: 'But I can't eat it . . . It's covered—with blood.'

Day Six:

THURSDAY, 21 DECEMBER, 1944

*'That place is very strong. I don't think the troops we have—
without further improvement—can take the thing.'*

General Harrison to General Hobbs,
C.O. 30th U.S. Infantry Division.

At noon in the Château du Froide Cour Peiper was
talking over the radio to an SS officer some fifteen miles away on
the heights overlooking the battered town of Stavelot, where
during the night a young American officer had risked his life to
blow up the middle span of the vital bridge. Now Peiper's major
lifeline was definitely cut.

'We're in a very bad condition,' he said, 'Very urgently need
Otto. Without Otto can't do anything.'

At the other end, the listener indicated that he understood and
would try to break through with 'Otto'. But it was very difficult.
He had suffered a lot of casualties attacking the bridge at
Stavelot. 'We will do what we can,' he concluded and signed off.

Peiper handed the earphones back to the operator. For a
moment he stood in the candle-lit cellar and stared blankly at the
wall, oblivious of the worried looks of the staff. Without 'Otto'
—fuel—he was finished, immobilized on the twin hilltops of
Stoumont and La Gleize, waiting for the *Amis* to put the final
squeeze on him. Admittedly a few litres of gasoline had come
floating down the river, placed in the Amblève at Stavelot by
Sandig, and a truck had sneaked through with several score
jerricans over the Petit-Spai bridge. But now the American
armour was reported to be blocking that source too.

Suddenly Peiper shook his head, as if to shake away the unpleasant thoughts which plagued him, then mounted the stairs to the room in which he had called a conference for noon.

His commanders were waiting for him, Diefenthal, Knittel, Gruhle, Sickel and the rest. As was his usual tactic in tough situations like this, he gave them the bad news first: they were virtually surrounded, their supplies were dreadfully low, especially gasoline. However, he continued, the Group had managed to throw back all efforts of the *Amis* to attack La Gleize from the east and the west and so far no threat had developed from the south. Then he paused and allowed himself a slight smile. 'But gentlemen,' he said carefully, 'the Divisional Commander has assured me that we will be relieved.' Swiftly he repeated what General Mohnke had told him over the radio that morning. With *his third and fourth march groups* in the area of Stavelot and east of Trois Ponts, he would advance on to the north bank of the Amblève and strike north-west or cross the Salm and then turn north.

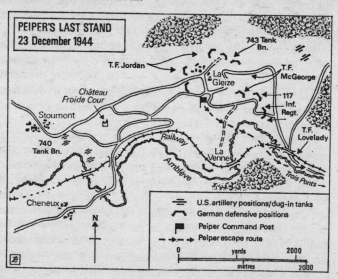

Peiper paused for a moment and allowed the news to sink in, gratified to see the slow light of hope spring into the tired eyes of his officers. Then he quickly outlined his own personal contribution to that operation. He would pull out all remaining German troops from Stoumont, evacuate his own command post of Château du Froide Cour, leaving behind those too badly wounded to walk, and concentrate in the hilltop village of La Gleize, but retaining his bridgehead at Cheneux. While his officers nodded their heads approvingly, he concluded that this new arrangement with a tight defensive perimeter around La Gleize and the bridgehead at Cheneux would enable him to fight on much longer, even though he was virtually immobilized from the lack of fuel—after all this was going to be an infantry battle —and at the same time he would retain a bridgehead for the resumption of the armoured advance westwards once Mohnke had reached him with supplies. A new enthusiasm made itself felt in the cold room. The young officers seized on the possibilities offered by this plan. Eagerly they began to ask questions. 'Who was going to look after the wounded? What about the *Ami* prisoners? When would they start the pull-back? Who would go first? How would they get the order to the men in the sanatorium . . . ?' Thus they questioned and counter-questioned their commander, standing before the map, suddenly strangely silent. For Peiper realised he had made them believe in something he no longer believed in himself.

The Ardennes Offensive had been going badly for the 6th Panzer Army Commander Sepp Dietrich. Right from the beginning he had not believed in Hitler's long-term objective— Antwerp; he knew that his undersupplied Army could never capture that major supply port. But he had believed in the short-term objective—the crossing of the Meuse and possibly a link-up with the troops scheduled to attack downwards from Holland. And he had set his hopes on Peiper being able to obtain the Meuse bridges for him. But the *Ami* defence of the Elsenborn Ridge had prevented his expansion of the original point of break-through. Accordingly he could neither support Peiper with the requisite follow-up armour nor ensure his supply lines.

Now Kraemer was worrying him with the possibility that Peiper would soon turn north to protect his endangered flank and line of communication. If this were the case, what could he put in the line to protect that flank? There was the 3rd Parachute Division located in a blocking position south of Waimes. But if he took it out of the line to help Peiper, the road would be open for *Ami* reinforcements from the north to reach St Vith, which must soon fall under the pressure of three and a half divisions.

The truth was that his Sixth Army had failed in its initial mission of opening a gap wide enough to send in major units in the second wave. So what he could do under the present circumstances was very little, save to ask the Luftwaffe, of which he thought very little, to airdrop supplies to Peiper and insist that Mohnke get himself off his backside and break through to Peiper with the rest of the 1st SS Panzer.

Thus immersed in his thoughts, he was startled by a knock on the door. It was Kraemer and the Army's Intelligence Officer.

'What is it?' Dietrich barked.

'This has just come through from *Soldatensender Calais*,'[1] Kraemer said and nodded to the Intelligence Chief.

The latter passed the flimsy to Dietrich. He took it impatiently and glanced over it; then he read again—this time more slowly. When he looked up, his face was drained of colour too. He knew what it meant. 'I want an investigation at once!' he said.

Kraemer nodded his agreement. 'Yes, sir, I think you're right. I'll see to it immediately.'

He went out, accompanied by the Intelligence Officer, leaving Dietrich staring down at the flimsy piece of paper which he knew was Peiper's death warrant, and probably his own too, since he was Peiper's commander, if they were ever captured by the *Amis*.

[1] A BBC propaganda station, conducted by the British journalist Sefton Delmer, who had been Berlin correspondent of the *Daily Express* prior to the war and directed his propaganda specifically at the German soldier, using mainly German POWs as broadcasters.

'In an attack to regain ground near the crossroads close to Thirimont south of Malmédy, about sixty dead American soldiers have been found. According to reports from their comrades who got away, they were shot by the enemy as they were surrendering or had already surrendered.'[1]

2

By early afternoon General Mohnke, commander of the 1st SS, was moving his men across the Amblève between Trois Ponts and Stavelot. Under the command of Colonel Hansen, a much-decorated veteran, the 1st Panzer Grenadier Regiment crossed at Petit-Spai and the Colonel established his command post three hundred yards away from the light bridge the regiment had used to cross, hidden from Task Force Lovelady by the dense fog.

Slowly his men began to grope their way forward towards their objective, La Gleize, advancing like packs of wolves through the thick rolling clouds of fog which deadened the sound of their approach.

To their front along an 8,000 yard line reaching from Trois Ponts south to Grand Halleux, the 505th Parachute Infantry of the 82nd Airborne waited for them, crouched in their snow-filled foxholes. All morning fleeing civilians had been passing through their lines bringing word of the German build-up. Somewhere out in the fog they could hear the sound of tracks. There was no mistaking it. German tanks were somewhere out there, looking for them.

Suddenly, out of the fog, they came. Unaware of the presence of the paratroopers, the German infantry followed their heavily-camouflaged vehicles at a half crouch. The tanks rumbled along the road parallel to the rise held by the Americans.

[1] In fact, the bodies of the 'Malmédy Massacre' victims were not recaptured until 14 Jan, 1945 when they were discovered by the advancing Americans under a thick layer of frozen snow.

It was too tempting a target for the nearest bazooka crew to resist. They fired without hesitation. The first SP disappeared in a cloud of smoke. The eight-man crew of the bazooka had struck lucky. Their next shot hit its target squarely and brought the vehicle to a halt. And then the next too. But that was it. The German infantry, enraged by the sudden American attack on their little force, swung out and hit the enemy line. Within a matter of minutes every one of the Americans was dead or taken prisoner.

But the howitzers of the 456th Parachute Field Artillery had heard the sound of the firing. Shooting blindly through the fog, they plastered the German positions and for a brief while disorganised the leading group.

On the German side of the river, the commander of the 2nd Battalion of the 505th Airborne, Colonel Vandervoort desperately tried to reach regimental headquarters over the radio phone. He was, it seemed, trapped in his little bridgehead across the river. What was he to do? His attempts to get through were unsuccessful and he realised that he would have to make his own decisions. Quickly he sent his F Company to climb the river bank that rose almost sheer at this point. They were followed by a lone 57 mm anti-tank gun, towed by a jeep driven by Lieutenant Jake Wurtrich.

German tanks appeared almost immediately, and Wurtrich braked hard. The crew baled out. Frantically they scrambled to unhook the gun, with the rumble of tanks getting ever closer, and swung the gun round, with a corporal hanging over the barrel to raise the trails in the air. With a clang the trails were snapped apart. Wurtrich flung himself between them. Opposite him, the loader rammed open the breech, thrust in the shell, closed the breech and Wurtrich fired. It was a hit, but the little six-pound shell bounced off like a ball, not even denting the thick frontal armour of the leading tank. Wurtrich fired again with the same result. The shell went whizzing off at a tangent to disappear somewhere in the trees. Wurtrich pressed his eye to the rubber eye-piece again. Another hit—and again the shell bounced off harmlessly. Then the gun of the leading tank fired and the little anti-tank gun flew apart, leaving Jake Wurtrich sprawled dead beside it. The American line began to break. They were suffering severe casualties and men were repeatedly leaving the line to take the wounded down the cliff.

Over on the other side, Colonel Ekman, the Regimental Commander had arrived. Together with Colonel Vandervoort, he decided to risk a manoeuvre which all staff colleges frowned upon—a day-light withdrawal. At first the withdrawal started well enough. But then the Germans sensed that their opponents were pulling back. They pressed home their advantage recklessly. The Americans' pace quickened. Men started to throw themselves off the cliff into the water and scramble back as best they could. Now everything was confusion and panic. The Germans were in among the fleeing paratroopers. A group swung itself across the river along the remains of one of the bridges. Another followed it, on the heels of the Americans. It looked as if the Germans had broken through on the Amblève.

Then suddenly the steam went out of the German attack. The bridge which Mohnke was using to back up his attack with armour, collapsed suddenly after only a handful of armoured vehicles had managed to get across. Frantically he called for his combat engineers, telling their commander he must get the bridge up regardless of losses.

The young engineer did his best, but hardly had his men managed to struggle into the waist-deep water, which ran very fast at this particular spot, and get their life-lines out, when American artillery zeroed in on them. For a while they stuck it, but after a score of men had been wounded or killed, the survivors pulled out, hoping that the fog would soon thicken again and allow them to get on with the job.

With their armour cut off, the infantry attack on the Amblève line began to weaken. The two platoons of infantry which had managed to follow up the retreat of the 2nd Battalion were mown down by men of the newly re-established line. To their south, the four large armoured vehicles which had crossed the now destroyed bridge were knocked out by paratroopers armed with gammon grenades.

By late afternoon it was all over for that day. The German attack to relieve Peiper had been stopped, though the 82nd's front was very weak indeed and there was no guarantee that the Germans might not breach it as soon as they had built up their strength. But for the time being Peiper was still cut off and immobilized, at the mercy of Harrison's infantry and tanks.

3

Harrison had scheduled his own counter-attack on Stoumont for the morning of the 21st at 0730, but the surprise German attack during the night had hit his 1st Battalion badly and he had been forced to postpone his move until 1245. Now the revised midday plan envisaged a three-battalion attack. Two of these would launch a holding attack, covered by Berry's tanks to the west, with Herlong's 1st Battalion scheduled to take the sanatorium. In the meantime Major McCown's 2nd Battalion, which was in the best shape, was to circle cross-country and cut the road east of Stoumont.

After a preliminary artillery bombardment, the Americans went up the battle-littered hill once more. At first the two-battalion attack made progress. Harrison's efforts were having an effect. Slowly but definitely the Americans fought their way up the hill. Pushing hard, they entered the sanatorium yet again and proceeded to clear the ground floor of the shattered building. But just when it appeared that they were getting the upper hand, the Germans pulled the same trick as on the day before. A Tiger rumbled up to the far side of the building, poked its gun through a window and began to blast away. The GIs looked for a means of escape. Their officers hesitated for a moment, but it was long enough. The first of the waverers were beginning to drop out of the windows on the far side and take off over the fields.

The attack stalled. It was no use. The NCOs and officers screamed, pleaded and threatened. The men would not move forward. The senior officer then called for smoke and under its cover, the infantry withdrew the way they had come, leaving the hillside littered with their dead.

Down below panic reigned among the civilians as an American tank-destroyer pounded the sanatorium's walls at 150 yards range to cover the infantry's retreat. The gunner's aim was deadly. He was still being supplied with directions from the Americans holed up in the annexe, who were defying all the enemy's attempts to throw them out.

Finally a shell penetrated the granite walls of the ground floor and brought down chunks of ceiling on the terrified civilians huddled in the cellar. Father Hanlet, saw that he must act if he were to prevent a stampede for the door. 'I will give you all General Absolution', he cried above the noise.

They knelt and in an almost unintelligible jabber followed him in the Act of Contrition. Then, just as Father Hanlet was about to ask God's pardon for all their sins, there was a frightening rushing sound and the huge sigh of a shell swallowing air. Next moment a shell crashed through the roof of the cellar itself. Acrid smoke filled the room. Father Hanlet fought his way to the stairs, hoping to get the Americans and Germans to declare a truce while he evacuated his flock. As his head emerged from the cellar, a German pressed the trigger of his machine pistol. There was a rapid burr of fire and Father Hanlet fell back down the cellar-steps. To his amazement, he was untouched. He staggered back to where his frightened people were waiting for him. 'Keep calm,' he gasped, 'I promise no evil will come to you.' Thinking he had spoken with the men fighting above their heads, the civilians calmed down. And amazingly, as if the priest had planned it, the firing began to die down.

Wiping his sweating brow, Father Hanlet looked up. In the flickering light of the candles, he could see the shell which had penetrated the cellar roof. It had not exploded, but was lodged there threateningly. Lowering his eyes quickly so that the others wouldn't follow the direction of his gaze, he whispered a quick prayer to God that it might be a dud.

While the fight was still raging at the sanatorium, McCown was leading his battalion in the swing round the town and his advance was going well. Without any trouble he managed to cut the main Stoumont-La Gleize road. But by early afternoon he was worried about the lack of contact with the other two regiments. Telling his second-in-command to get the men working on a road-block at the most likely spot, he set off with his runner and a radio operator to have a look at the situation himself. Before he made his next move, he wanted to be sure of his position. This was the first battalion command and although he had been lucky in yesterday's fighting on the river, he didn't want to chance his luck any further.

Moving out into the broken hilly country to the front of his right company, he suddenly spotted three Germans from what looked at that distance like a combat patrol. McCown reacted almost instinctively. The first man dropped, riddled by a burst from the officer's burp gun. The other two ducked behind some bushes. McCown's mind raced. Should he go after them for further information? Or should he take off the way he had come? The enemy made up his mind for him. Small arms fire came from two directions. McCown crouched next to his two men, his machine pistol ready for quick action. But now his luck had deserted him.

'*Kommen Sie hierher!*' a harsh voice said to his rear. McCown swung round, machine pistol coming up into the firing position. Then his mouth fell open and the pistol sank quickly.

A long line of armed Germans were covering the little group of Americans. McCown dropped his weapons and raised his hands. His two companions watched him in shocked silence; then they too followed his example. The Commander of the 2nd Battalion, 119th Infantry, was a prisoner of war.

While his leaderless battalion faded away, returning to their start positions, McCown was led to Stoumont where he was interrogated by a lieutenant-colonel, who soon lost interest when McCown stuck to his name, number and rank. He was passed on to a group of junior officers and finally to some NCOs, but although their threats were less subtle than those of the officers, McCown stuck to his initial statement. Finally they left him in peace and he was taken to a cellar near Monsieur Natalis' schoolhouse. Coming to the conclusion that the safest place in the badly-lit room was with his back to the wall, he settled down and to his amazement discovered a bookshelf just above his head. Picking a book at random, he found it was a copy of E. Philips Oppenheim's *Great Impersonation*. As best as he could in the dim light, he began to read about the exploits of Oppenheim's unlikely upper-class characters acting out their roles in a world so far removed from his own at present as was the moon.

That December day brought little news of any comfort for the Americans fighting on the Amblève River front. The only bright spot in the whole black firmament was the action at Cheneux. There the exhausted gliderborne infantry had pulled themselves together during the early hours of the morning and had gone tank-hunting in the village, armed with knife and grenade. Taking and giving heavy casualties, they captured the German flak wagons, which had inflicted so much punishment on them during their initial attack

In one case Staff Sergeant Bill Walsh was leading a platoon when it was pinned down by flanking fire from one of the remaining flak wagons. Although he himself was so badly wounded that a member of his squad had to arm the grenade for him, he rushed the German crew and blew them up.

When morning came, General Gavin turned the whole regiment over to Colonel Tucker, giving him the simple order to 'wipe out the Krauts'. Realising the vital importance of the task which had been assigned to his regiment, Colonel Tucker sent Colonel Julian Cook's 1st Battalion in a wide flanking movement over rough country that took six hours. Taking the Germans by surprise, the 1st Battalion had them beaten by the late afternoon.

Few Germans survived the battle and their dead lay scattered in the ruined village. Considerable booty was taken too, including 14 flak wagons and a battery of 105 mm howitzers, but the cost had been high—225 dead and wounded. Out of the two assault companies, Company B had 18 men left and no officers while Company C had 38 men and 3 officers.

Yet back at his headquarters near Werbomont, Ridgway, when informed of the news, felt the price was justified. It was one more step on the way that Montgomery had prescribed for his Corps. The last remaining German bridgehead outside of La Gleize–Stoumont was taken. Even if Mohnke did manage to break through to Peiper, there was no longer a bridge to take them westwards to the Meuse.

Otherwise the situation was blacker than when the day had started. Earlier Hobbs, the Divisional Commander of the 30th Infantry Division, had assured Ridgway that if the 82nd Airborne cleared the south bank of the Amblève, he would need no further help; they could get on with their mission of relieving St Vith and helping to get the besieged garrison out. But now the Germans were making their presence felt in a decidedly aggressive manner both at La Gleize–Stoumont and on the river itself at Petit-Spai. It hardly seemed possible but one German SS division was taking on an airborne division, one regiment of infantry and one of armour, and that with their supplies cut off!

In exasperation Hobbs called Harrison just as it was getting dark and the fighting was dying away for another day. 'I want to know the real picture down there?' he said to his assistant. General Harrisons' answer was frankly pessimistic. His 1st and 3rd Battalions had been badly hit and were demoralised. They gave easily and were 'in pretty bad shape'.

Asked about his armour under Berry, Harrison replied that 'The trouble is the only places where tanks of any kind can operate are on two sunken roads. The Germans have big tanks, so tanks have been no help to us'.

Then came the question of what action he would take on the morrow. Again Harrison was pessimistic. He told Hobbs he was against continuing the attack. 'That place is very strong. I don't think the troops we have now, without some improvement, can take the thing.' Harrison was depressed and he was not going to lie, even if it cost him his command. 'That's my honest opinion. They are way down in strength. The trouble is that we can only get light artillery fire on the town, and the Germans can shoot at us with tank guns and we can't get tanks to shoot back unless they come out and get hit.'

Hobbs listened in silence to his subordinate's gloomy picture. He knew how in combat the worm's eye view often predominated and the man on the spot usually over-exaggerated the difficulties he was facing. But Harrison was an experienced officer who had been with him since Normandy and was not given to over-doing it.

Hobbs contented himself with warning Harrison to be on the look-out for a German attempt to break out during the night and head west. Obviously he was unaware of Peiper's acute shortage of fuel. Then he tried to cheer Harrison up, telling him he would work out something with Ridgway to get a group from the 82nd Airborne to attack the southern side of the Stoumont– La Gleize pocket. With that he signed off. But Harrison's answers to his questions had had their effect. He knew the Shermans' weaknesses well; mostly their crews were frightened to venture out in their 'Ronsons', where even a near miss in the engine section would send the tank's highly sensitive gasoline motor up in flames. And, unable to bring artillery to bear and without tank support, Harrison wouldn't be able to get his infantry to advance, especially as American infantry had been trained to expect air, artillery or tank support before they went into action.

The General considered the problem for a while, then he made his decision. He called Ridgway. Ridgway had had a bad day.

His front was being broken everywhere, and now it looked as if St Vith would fall at any moment. But he listened patiently to the 30th Division commander as he explained his problem and then asked him what he wanted to recommend. Under the circumstances, Hobbs said, he recommended an all-out air attack on Peiper, as it appeared that the weather would be suitable for flying on the following day—the first such day since the start of the German attack. Ridgway agreed and Hobbs said that he 'could use up to sixteen groups in one day' and that his own air support officer would have the targets ready.

There the matter rested. Everything else had failed; so the U.S. Army would call in the might of its air arm to dislodge the stubborn Peiper from his hilltop fortress. Now everything depended on the weather.

4

By late afternoon Peiper had pulled back his perimeter, taking with him all walking wounded and prisoners, leaving the rest in the charge of a German sergeant and two American medics. Now the force began to concentrate in and around La Gleize. The village consisted of two streets—the upper one, close to the road to Trois Ponts, on which were a few houses and a couple of modest hotels, and the lower one around the church and village square, with its bistro, priest's house and village school. Here Peiper took up his quarters in the cellar. Already American artillery was beginning to pound the village with a bombardment which was to continue right to the end of Peiper's defence.

Hal McCown, the senior American prisoner, was in a cellar adjoining the school, reading his novel as best he could in the bad light. Around him four young lieutenants from other battalions of the 119th sprawled on the floor and tried to sleep under the lazy gaze of four guards. Almost unconsciously he noticed the heightened rate of artillery fire and felt it getting closer. The book trembled in his hand every time one of the shells landed close by. He looked up at his guards. They didn't seem to notice. He would pretend not to notice either. He went on reading.

Suddenly there was a huge crump, followed by a violent explosion. The wall above McCown's head bulged inwards. He fell to the floor, momentarily stunned. When he came to, he found he couldn't move. Then he saw the reason. One of the guards lay motionless across him. Around him most of the others were either dead or wounded. Desperately he struggled free, sweating under the weight of the wounded German.

Towards midnight a guard entered the cellar, still strewn with the dead and wounded, and escorted McCown across the road to Peiper's command post. Steeling himself, he prepared his mind to limit itself to the same old trinity: name, number and rank: no more, no less. But he was in for a surprise, as he was ushered into the presence of the commander of the *Kampfgruppe*. Peiper had seemingly given up his attempt to get any information out of his senior American prisoner. For some reason he appeared just to want to talk, almost as if he were lonely and were seeking companionship. In later years McCown was often to wonder why Peiper had him brought out that night; perhaps he had something of that German *Seele* in him which demands that it must explain itself in detail.

Thus began a long talk that rambled on and on in the gray little cellar, with the regular thump of the American shells landing outside acting like a kind of punctuation during which the loquacious German was forced to be silent.

McCown was struck by the man's fanaticism. Peiper was all that he had been taught to expect from a Nazi soldier. After observing that 'We can't lose. Himmler's new reserve army has so many new divisions your G-2s will wonder where they came from,' he went on to talk in general about his devotion to the Nazi cause. 'Oh, I admit many wrongs have been committed. But we think of the great good Hitler is accomplishing. We're eliminating the Communist menace, fighting *your* fight. And the Fuehrer's concept of a unified, more productive Europe! Can't

11. American infantrymen in Bastogne, December, 1944

12. Men of the 117th Infantry Regiment, 30th Division, approaching St. Vith, January, 1945

13. A Supply Convoy moving through Bastogne, January, 1945

you see what good that will bring? We will keep what is best in Europe and eliminate the bad.'

Warming to his theme, he went on eagerly to describe the enthusiasm with which the German invaders had been received in the other European countries. Everywhere millions of non-Germans—French, Belgians, Dutch, Norwegians and Finns—had accepted the Fuehrer's idea of 'One Europe', joined in common cause against the Soviet menace. McCown did not know it then, but Peiper had swallowed hook, line and sinker the last great Goebbelian propaganda line, which replaced the old 'Germanic' concept when it was realised that Germany was losing the war, the idea of a West European 'crusade' against the sub-human Russian.

Yet if McCown did not know the source of Peiper's enthusiastic 'crusade', he did comprehend the German's fanaticism and sincerity. Amazingly enough as the night turned into dawn, he began to find his initial reserve turning into a kind of sympathy. The young German colonel, who was only a couple of years older than himself but who had seen so much more of war, was a person of humour and culture and obviously highly intelligent, much more so than many a comparable officer in the American Army. While he listened, McCown asked himself how a man of such high calibre could ever believe the crude Nazi lies.

But he was primarily concerned with the safety of the one hundred and fifty POWs that Peiper had under his command. By now he was fairly certain that this was the man whose outfit had reportedly shot a large number of unarmed Americans after they had surrendered at Baugnez, and he was worried what might happen, especially as the swaggering, somewhat hysterical young soldiers he had been seeing all day did not impress him as being very stable. He kept his own counsel and asked about the notoriously ruthless treatment of Russian prisoners taken in the East.

Peiper smiled: 'I'd like to take you to the Eastern Front,' he said enthusiastically. 'Then you'd see why we've had to violate all the rules of warfare. The Russians have no idea what the

Geneva Convention means. Some day, perhaps, you Americans will find out for yourselves. And you'll have to admit our behaviour on the Western Front has been very correct.'

Feeling more confident about Peiper now, McCown continued to press for an assurance that nothing would happen to the captive Americans. 'Colonel Peiper,' he said, 'will you give your personal assurance that you'll abide by the rules of Land Warfare?'

Peiper looked at him solemnly: 'You have my word,' he answered.

It had been a long night, and all the two men had had to keep them awake were a couple of cups of ersatz coffee. But McCown was feeling better now than at any time since he had been captured. He had spent the small hours digging Peiper for information, and the latter had rambled on in his excellent English about the new wonder weapons the Fuehrer had promised the German People and how the German attack would soon be as far forward as the vital supply port. But it was apparent to McCown that Peiper no longer believed in a German victory. He was doing a job and doing it damned well, as was to be expected of a good soldier. And in addition to the fact that Peiper no longer believed in the cause for which he was fighting so hard, and that meant to McCown that the whole Nazi structure must be rotten if such a man had resigned himself to defeat, he was now pretty sure that Peiper would honour his promise not to harm the prisoners.[1]

Now the first light of dawn was beginning to creep through the cracks in the cellar door. Up above there was the sound of heavy boots stamping across the stone flags. From somewhere there was the rattle of mess tins and the smell of coffee. The volume of fire started to increase. A fresh day of war had dawned. Peiper looked at his watch and then called for a guard. He smiled momentarily at his prisoner and then motioned to the guard to take McCown away. There was the business of war to be attended to.

[1] In the whole three and a half days of his captivity, McCown observed only one breach of the Geneva Convention—when Peiper ordered some POWs to load trucks under fire, though Peiper did tell him that he had been forced to shoot seven prisoners who had tried to escape.

Day Seven:
FRIDAY, 22 DECEMBER, 1944

*'Let everyone hold before him a single thought—to destroy
the enemy on the ground, in the air, everywhere—destroy
him!'*

General Eisenhower, Order
of the Day, 22 December, 1944.

James Berry crept cautiously out of the snow-laden firs.
His body held tense and expectant, he crouched there for an
instant, waiting for the sudden hard blow which would indicate
that the enemy had spotted him. But none came. He relaxed
a little. What the hell had made him volunteer for this one-man
reconnaissance job? He could have detailed one of his men
to go.

His hand slid down to his pistol to reassure himself for the
nth time that it was still there. He bit his upper lip and concentrated on the task before him. His eyes swept the ground to
his front. No sign of sentries. The shattered sanatorium lay
silent and peaceful, its outline clearly defined against the
night sky. Cautiously he took a step forward. Below his boots
the frozen snow crunched alarmingly. He stopped and cocked
his head to one side. No sound save the ever-present rumble of
heavy artillery a long way off. He went on. Captain Berry's
task that bitterly cold night was to find out whether it was
possible to build a ramp over the 'fill', or embankment, which
up to now had barred direct assault on the sanatorium. If it

were, then he could move up his Shermans and let the defenders have it at direct range.

He moved on. Now he was in front of the 'fill.' He forgot his fear, concentrating on the technical task facing him. Could the Shermans make it? Quickly he moved to the left and had a look at the embankment from that angle. Yes, he thought, they could. If his boys could build a ramp up to it or over it, they'd be able to get the Shermans within short range of the sanatorium. Satisfied that he had completed his task, Berry sneaked back the way he had come. Once in the trees, he blundered on hurriedly, careless of the noise now, free of danger, like a schoolboy released after some particularly difficult examination.

By midnight, his volunteers were hard at work, building the ramp from shell casings, while behind them the first four Shermans were ready and waiting, their engines ticking over gently. Soon the attack could start.

The four Shermans went into action just before dawn. Several miles to the rear a great 155 mm cannon joined the bombardment. Under the direct fire of American tanks, the building slowly began to crumble. The roof came crashing down with a great roar. Yet still the handful of SS left behind, possibly because they had not received Peiper's withdrawal order, clung to their precarious hold on the strongpoint.

But they were at the end of their tether. Ammunition was running low and they were almost out of food. This continuous bombardment, especially the direct fire from the Shermans, which they had never thought could get that close, was wearing them down rapidly.

Above them, the civilians could hear the Germans dragging their surviving cannon into position to face the tanks. With a crash the gun opened fire. The SS were going to make a fight of it. The battle raged back and forth around the ruined sanatorium. Down below the cellar ceiling swayed and threatened to come crashing down everytime the German gun fired.

Father Hanlet folded his hands in prayer. That was the only hope left for him and his flock now.

The fight at the sanatorium lasted for an hour. Then suddenly the German gun fell silent. Above them the surviving Germans had sneaked away. The civilians dropped into an uneasy sleep, but not for long. Again there came the sound of violent firing close at hand. Father Hanlet looked up at the swaying ceiling and realised that it wouldn't last much longer. He called the nuns to him and explained that they must get the people out of the cellar. Battle or no battle, they could not stay there.

At once the 'white swans' started to go from bed to bed, waking the exhausted children, while Father Hanlet followed them giving Holy Communion to those who wished it, as they knelt, hands clasped, before their grubby mattresses.

The Mother Superior with another nun and the gardener volunteered to go upstairs with a white flag and try to get them to safety. Seconds later another violent barrage shook the building. The ceiling heaved and swayed; dust poured from the cracks; huge pieces of plaster came tumbling down; it seemed as if it must cave in at any moment.

Another 'white' flag was made from a dirty tablecloth and an American soldier, wounded in the knee, volunteered to take it and try to get them out. Hobbling badly, he went up the stairs, holding the flag. He vanished into the darkness and never came back.

But a few minutes later an excited villager clattered down the stairs, crying, 'The soldiers want two sisters or civilians to be *parlementaires!*'

'Are they German or American?'

The villager did not know, but Father Hanlet knew that this might be his last chance to get his people out. He nodded to a tiny nun who at once swept up the stairs, her big white hat flapping absurdly, followed by two civilians. Again there was a long wait and the firing went on.

Then the door of the cellar opened and a tired, unshaven American officer, carbine in hand, stood there staring at the terrified civilians. His face wore a broad smile. It was all over. 'You can all leave in a few minutes,' he said. Father Hanlet had saved his flock.

Now things began to get organised. Two stretcher-bearers came down the stairs and carefully lifted the man who had been badly wounded in the arm in the first attack on to the stretcher, the same man to whom Father Hanlet had given the last rites, two evenings before. Slowly the children began to file out and Father Hanlet followed. The first floor was a complete wreck. The walls were full of shell holes and everything had been reduced to a heap of rubble. Everywhere there were bodies, American and German, entwined in the nationless promiscuity of death. Father Hanlet surveyed the scene and bent his head in prayer while past him the children filed outside into the dawn.

The Battle for Stoumont was almost over.

Just outside the town, which patrols had reported strangely silent, General Harrison waited for the blizzard to stop. It had been snowing since dawn. Harrison took off his glasses and wiped away the snow, then stared at the hill which led into Stoumont. Around him the infantry blew on their fingers and stamped their frozen feet. A little to their rear, Berry's men revved their engines, trying to keep them warm for the moment of attack. And behind them the artillerymen fussed with their pieces, keeping the breeches free of snow, stacking more and more ammunition. Harrison knew that he would have to rely on his artillery; in this weather there was no hope of air support. The attack was due to go in at 1300; it was already noon and there was no sign of the storm abating.

Then slowly it seemed to ease; visibility increased. Harrison passed back his orders to the artillery. It was past one now. He must get moving. Both Hobbs and Ridgway had insisted on the utmost speed. At 1320 the artillery went into action. With a crash the shells landed on the outskirts of the village. The next salvo fell on target. Here and there one of the little houses went up in a cloud of smoke and flame.

But the enemy wasn't beaten yet. Just as the NCO's and officers of the lead company began to chivvy their men into position, there was the familiar sound of an 88 mm. Harrison ducked instinctively. So did the infantry. The Germans had zeroed in on the assembly area. Shells began to fall everywhere.

Harrison was determined to continue the attack; indeed with Hobbs and Ridgway breathing down his neck he had no alternative. Knowing the Germans to be desperately short of ammunition, he ordered the artillery barrage to stop, thereby hoping to persuade the enemy to do the same. The trick worked. He looked at the infantry. They didn't look too good, but they were all he had. He nodded. The 3rd Battalion started to move out in a long thin line, picking their way forward in silence, weapons held across their chests, edging in little groups closer and closer to the protecting metal of the rumbling tanks.

Harrison followed them with his glasses. They were getting close to the first houses now. At any moment the German machine-gunners would open up, and the first line would go down in a mess of sprawling bodies. But nothing happened. He watched the men's pace quicken. An officer turned and waved his hand to the tanks. In a Sherman a man stood up and gave the hand signal to advance. The tanks rumbled forward awkwardly. Now the infantry had disappeared in among the houses. The tanks followed. Harrison let his glasses fall. They had made it. His men were in Stoumont!

Like the men who had attacked the sanatorium, the 3rd Battalion found that Stoumont was occupied only by the wounded and by civilians. Those Germans who were left were dying. Swiftly the Americans spread out, advancing steadily up the hill, combing the shattered houses for their own wounded who had been left behind and any Germans who had been abandoned during the retreat.

As always Monsieur Natalis was waiting for them, but this time he had restrained his natural curiosity enough to remain in the cellar of the house of his neighbour, Doctor Robinson.

The Americans reached the house in the mid-afternoon. They went down into the cellar suspiciously, rifles held at the ready. 'There is no one but civilians here in the cellar,' the little teacher said hastily in English, pointing to his three companions. The leading American obviously took Natalis for a German, mistaking his pronunciation of 'cellar' for the German word '*Keller*'. Quickly Natalis produced a bottle of wine and opened it, offering the soldiers some. They forced him to drink the first glass himself, then began to drink heartily. Natalis smiled and left them to it, his chronic curiosity taking him out of the cellar to see what was happening in the village. Later when he returned to his own house, he discovered his whole supply of wine had disappeared. Ruefully he concluded that it was part of the price of victory.

2

General Priess, the commander of the 1 SS Panzer Corps, to which Peiper's *Kampfgruppe* belonged, had had a hard morning He had been trying to convince Dietrich and Kraemer that they should pull Peiper out while he still had the strength to fight his way east to his own lines. But although his suggestion had gone the whole way to the High Command in Berlin it had been turned down. In spite of the growing strength of the Americans on the northern flank the Berlin generals remained convinced that the build-up would not reach the danger mark until their own armoured divisions had reached and crossed the Meuse. A warning from the father of the panzer division, Colonel General Heinz Guderian himself, had equally little effect. General Guderian argued that if the German armoured divisions were not withdrawn from the Ardennes, where the offensive was obviously slowing down, there would be nothing left to meet the Russian offensive in the East which he expected to be launched at any time. But neither Hitler nor Himmler would listen to him, the latter saying airily, 'You know, my dear

Colonel General, I don't really believe the Russians will attack at all. It's all an enormous bluff. I'm convinced there's nothing going on in the East.'

So there the matter rested. All that Priess could get out of Dietrich was the promise to have the Luftwaffe drop supplies to Peiper during the night of the 22nd. He would have to hold out until such time as reinforcements reached him from the second wave of German armour. Priess gave up in disgust, knowing in his own mind that Peiper was being sacrificed for an objective that was no longer realistic.

In La Gleize itself Peiper's situation continued to deteriorate rapidly, though he did not yet know that he had been virtually written off by the command of the 6th Panzer Army. In fact, he had hardly any way of knowing what was going on outside his own little fortress since his transmitters were only working intermittently and all that Mohnke saw fit to relay to him that day were nagging bureaucratic orders asking why he was not reporting the location of his position, though, in fact, his superiors knew his position quite well thanks to the extremely careless US radio nets which were a constant source of information to them throughout the battle. One order in particular raised Peiper's blood pressure to boiling point in view of the fact that he no longer had sufficient gas to charge his radio batteries. It read: 'Unless you report the amount of gas still on hand, you cannot hope for any additional gasoline.'[1]

But Peiper had other, more pressing, problems on hand. The Americans were beginning to filter into the thirty odd houses of the little town; fighting was breaking out everywhere, and the village was being rocked by a continuous artillery bombardment, directed, he presumed, from his old CP at the Château du Froide Cour. In addition large numbers of the enemy were advancing on him from two directions: Harrison's 119th Infantry from Stoumont and Task Force McGeorge from

---

[1] After the war when Peiper was asked by military intelligence what would he do if he were to conduct the Ardennes operation again, he gave as his Point No. 8: 'Put a general at each street corner to regulate traffic'.

the 3rd Armored coming down the valley road east of La Gleize. Hastily he sent what tanks still had fuel to stop both advances and these succeeded in bringing the *Amis* to a halt, Task Force McGeorge losing two tanks in the process.

Once that threat had been overcome, Peiper began to take stock of his situation. His supply route was cut off and Mohnke's promised relief seemed to be as far away as ever. Admittedly there was still the sound of firing coming from the direction of the Amblève, but whether it indicated that Mohnke was making any progress he did not know. He was inclined to believe that Mohnke's push had been halted; there seemed to be plenty of *Amis* between La Gleize and the river. Now for the first time, bottled up in the little hillside village, he was beginning to suffer really heavy casualties, most of them caused by the American artillery which gave him no peace. It seemed that it could only be a matter of time before the continuing American pressure wore him down. He paused and looked up at the sky. Today he had been lucky; the weather had been in his favour. But it seemed to be improving, and once the low cloud-base lifted, he knew the *Amis* would hit him with the whole weight of their air power. Then he was finished for good.

Suddenly Peiper made a decision. He hurried over to the radio car, praying that the operator would be able to raise Mohnke. He was lucky. In clear, Peiper put his decision to the Divisional Commander some twenty miles away. It was simple and direct: 'Almost all our Hermann[1] is gone. We have no Otto. It's just a question of time before we're completely destroyed. *Can we break out?*'

3

As dusk fell over the Ardennes that evening, it marked the end of the first week of the 'Battle of the Bulge', or the 'Rundstedt Offensive', as it was still being called in the British and

[1] Ammunition.

American papers. As yet none of Eisenhower's counter-measures were having any significant effect. In the south Patton had completed an amazing move, bringing three divisions from the Saar over a hundred miles of unfamiliar, ice-bound roads and into the battle dead on time. But so far his drive into the 'Bulge' had brought no appreciable results.

In the North, every division that Montgomery fed into the line was eaten up, drawn into the battle in pieces so that Ridgway's corps front, which stretched forty miles, had absorbed more divisions than he anticipated it should need. Nor could Montgomery yet convince the Americans, with their aggressive, almost neurotic, pre-occupation with ground, that they should withdraw if necessary, that the possession of ground *per se* meant very little.

In London the first signs were beginning to appear to the furore that Montgomery's appointment to the command of the northern sector eventually caused. Although the details of the appointment were not released until well into January when the danger was almost over, British newspapermen were already aware of what had happened at Versailles and by using the old trick of quoting 'German sources', and thus avoiding censorship, they implied that the British Field-Marshal had been forced to come to the rescue of the Americans because of Bradley's mismanagement of his armies. Soon the reports were to be picked up in America and become the cause of a major split between the Anglo-American allies.

In Paris, Eisenhower was a virtual prisoner of his own military police, who, scared by the rumours that Germans dressed in US uniforms and speaking fluent English would assassinate the Supreme Commander, had thrown an impenetrable ring around him. That day he managed to escape their scrutiny for a while and went out for a walk. Thus refreshed he returned and wrote one of his rare orders of the day. It read:

'By rushing out from his fixed defences the enemy may give us the chance to turn his great gamble into his worst defeat. So I call upon every man, of all the Allies, to rise now to new heights of resolution and of effort. Let everyone hold before him a single thought—to destroy the enemy on the ground, in the air, everywhere—destroy him! United in this determination and with unshakeable faith in the cause for which we fight, we will, with God's help, go forward to our greatest victory.'

The mood of panic in certain sections of the Supreme Headquarters was reflected everywhere in the rear areas that day. In Belgium and Luxemburg and Northern France an estimated 100,000 refugees were on the road again as in the bad days of May, 1940. The portraits of the Allied leaders which had decorated the windows of houses were taken down and many civilians avoided contact with the military, afraid that German sympathisers and spies would report such contacts once the Boche returned.

The military were little better. The big cities were filled with deserters who had 'bugged out' and were now trying to find some kind of hiding place with one of the wooden-shoed, bare-legged whores who flooded the bars frequented by the soldiers. In the replacement depots, the young soldiers, some of whom had only six weeks of basic training, were paraded in huge hastily-thrown-together companies—engineers, infantry, tankers all intermingled—and marched off to the waiting trucks, while behind them the permanent staff burned the secret documents and smashed bottle after bottle of beer and spirits against the walls so that the troops did not get their hands on them. And at every crossroads, suspicious soldiers stopped every truck, jeep and tank and subjected their occupants to a long-drawn examination. A spy scare of unprecedented dimensions had seized the rear areas.

In Luxemburg at Bradley's HQ, the daily target conference held in the Ninth Air Force's Advanced Headquarters War Room concluded with Major Stuart Fuller's statement that, 'For the next few days, there will be unrelieved gloom. No break can be expected until about 26 December.'

The gloom of that forecast spread over the whole front that snowy December day as dusk gave way to night. A week had gone by and still there seemed to be no end to the German drive forward. Far away from the front in a Washington that was still hot and stuffy in spite of the season, President Roosevelt refused to answer questions about the surprise German offensive, limiting himself to the statement that 'the end was not in sight' and those at home should exert every effort at this critical time to back up the men at the fighting front. In the Allied camp despondency settled down heavily on those who had to make the decisions which would shape the morrow.

Day Eight:
SATURDAY, 23 DECEMBER, 1944

'Permission or not, we're breaking out of here on foot!'
                    Colonel Peiper to his radio officer.

The day dawned cold, crisp and bright all over the Ardennes. Despite the dour predictions of the Ninth Air Force weathermen in Luxemburg the day before, the weather was perfect. For the first time since the start of the offensive, the weather was ideal for flying. Soon the 'phones at the 9th Air Force HQ began to ring, as harassed corps commanders seized the straw offered to them by the change in the weather and requested air strikes.

Behind the front, from airfields in France, Luxemburg and Belgium, the Mitchells, Flying Fortresses and Thunderbolts started to take off in their hundreds. In the cities and villages the people took to the streets, wakened out of an uneasy sleep by the unaccustomed noise. Craning their necks, they stared into the sky at the ever-growing armada of Allied planes speeding to the attack. The change in the weather had altered the whole course of the battle. From now until 27 December, when the back of the German attack was broken for good, the enemy was going to see one of the most striking demonstrations of Allied power in the air since the D-Day assault on the Normandy beaches.

But at the La Gleize sector of the front, General Harrison was still unaware of the change and the opportunities it offered him. He had had a bad night. Just after midnight, the air-raid warning had sounded all along the 30th–82nd Divisions front. Twenty-two Luftwaffe planes were reported over the American line. Troops had been put on the alert, and here and there parachutes were seen floating down. Most of them turned out to be supply 'chutes, with ammunition and gas attached to them, but immediately somebody at Corps Headquarters jumped to the conclusion that they were part of a paradrop to relieve Peiper. Rumour ran wild, with paratroopers being reported everywhere around La Gleize, and although General Hobbs told Corps that a paradrop made little sense in that area, Harrison's infantry had been on duty all night long.

Now Harrison was expected to send a force of infantry into the attack on La Gleize. He did not like it, but he knew time was running out. Already Ridgway was threatening to take his armour from him to be used elsewhere on his terribly over-extended front, forced by increasing German pressure at half-a-dozen different places. Wearily he gave out his orders.

This time the infantry would try a new approach. They would flank the village and move in from the woods to the north, their advance covered by forward artillery observers located very close to the target and directing cannon firing the new POZIT-fused shell. This was the proximity fuse, a tightly guarded American secret design for detonating shells by external influence in the close vicinity of the target, without explosion by contact. It was first used in the Ardennes and two days before had broken an attack by Colonel Skorzeny's 150th Brigade on Malmédy, with catastrophic casualties being inflicted upon the Germans.

In spite of the hope he held for the new weapon, Harrison was worried by the concentration of heavy tanks that Peiper still possessed in the centre of the village just by the church. What role were they to play in the defence? He was pretty sure that the Luftwaffe scare during the night had, in fact, been a para-drop for Peiper. If he had got his hands on sufficient quantities of fuel, would he now use his heavy tanks for some form of desperate counter-attack or break-through against which the tanks of the 740th Tank Battalion wouldn't stand a chance?

But while Harrison was debating the problem, the ground mist began to lift to reveal the clear winter sky. This was the opportunity he had been waiting for. Hurriedly he got on the phone. Minutes later he replaced the receiver, happy in the knowledge that his attack was going to be aided by an air strike on the village square. He had nothing more to fear from Peiper's Tigers and Panthers.

While Harrison prepared for the attack on La Gleize, six other rifle companies were already at work on the north bank of the Amblève, where the rest of the 1 SS Division, under Hanssen, still retained a foothold. The Germans were no longer concerned with attempting to relieve Peiper; now they were fighting desperately for their own lives, trying to hang on to what they had.

The fighting took place in the wooded area close to Stavelot, and it was tough and bitter, mostly carried out at close quarters. In one case two sergeants, Paul Bolden and Russel Snoad, decided that they would have to capture a German-held house which was holding up their company. While the men stayed under cover, Snoad sprayed the house with his 'grease gun', as Bolden edged his way closer and closer to it, noting the flashes of the enemy rifles. When he was in a position to attempt the last rush he turned and gave Snoad the signal that he was going to go in. Then he was up and running forward. He reached the door, drew the pin out of a grenade, counted a couple of seconds, flung open the door, threw it in and pulled the door shut. There was a thick muffled crump and he could feel the door pulsate under his hand. He opened it again. A wave of acrid smoke hit him in the face. A second grenade flew in. This time he did not close the door, but followed the grenade inside, firing his Tommy gun from the hip. Men started to fall all around him, but not before a shot from an upper window had killed Sgt Snoad. In the end Bolden cleared the house and

14. *Festung Sankt Edouard.* The T.B. Sanitorium at Stoumont today

15. The Chateau du Froide Cour

16. The Monument to the Malmédy Massacre at the Baugnez crossroads. The building on the right is the rebuilt Cafe Bodarwé. The stone in the foreground marks the furthest point of the German advance towards Malmédy itself.

17. The Bridge over the River Amblève at Stavelot as it looks today

stood panting at the door while the platoon filed by to count the dead. There were twenty in all[1].

But while the American troops on the Amblève were relatively successful that day, Harrison's attack was again doomed to failure. In the early afternoon the 113th Field Artillery, using the new POZIT-fuse, went into action. The result was predictable, as the proximity shell did its deadly work. The Germans fled to their cellars, leaving the streets empty except for the tanks.

The infantry started to move up, confident that the artillery had broken the back of the German resistance. Almost immediately the leading men ran into mines. It took only a couple of explosions and the whole point came to a stop, staring at the mutilated objects which had once been men, lying moaning in the bloodied snow.

The Shermans rattled over the ridge towards them, regardless of the mines. They would lead the advance. But the Germans were prepared for them as well. Just as the first Sherman breasted the minefield and prepared to move on, the well-dug-in Tigers opened up from their positions along the heights. The first Sherman went up in flames. Another came to an abrupt halt, its crew alive but trapped in the middle of the minefield. The rest turned tail and fled back to the cover of the other side of the ridge.

Now the artillery was called upon to blast the tanks while engineers moved up, crawling forward through the snow, trying to locate the mines. Thus it went on all afternoon, the advance stopping, waiting for the engineers and the artillery, and then moving on again, leaving behind them the steadily burning hulks of Shermans and the still figures in the snow.

By late afternoon they had fought their way to the outskirts of La Gleize, and the artillery was forced to cease firing in case they hit their own men. The first platoon was worming its way through the outlying houses when it was met by the fire of a four-barrel 20 mm flak cannon. The platoon took cover at

[1] For his action that day Bolden was awarded the Medal of Honor and Snoad the DSC posthumously.

once. Another cannon joined in, to be followed seconds later by heavy machine-guns. The American attack came to a halt, this time for good that day.

Harrison, in his CP at the Château du Froide Cour, looked anxiously at his watch when he heard that the advance had broken down. Now it was up to the Air Force. With their help he would be able to get things moving again. Both Hobbs and Ridgway were exerting pressure on him to take La Gleize by the end of the day. Without the Air Force it would be impossible. His men were exhausted and demoralised. General Harrison walked over to the window and stared up at the bright blue sky, still empty of planes.

At 1526 six B-29s of the 322nd US Bombardment Group of the 9th Air Force were flying in a gleaming silver V close to the German–Belgian border. Down below the flight leader had spotted a medium-sized cluster of houses in the centre of a hilly valley. He checked once again with his map. In spite of the excellent flying weather, he had not been able to find his primary target which had been the town of Zulpich in Germany. This town was supposed to be the railhead for General Branden-berger's Seventh Army, which had a defensive role in the Ardennes operation. But the young flight leader figured that the town down below must be Lammersum, some six miles north-east of his objective. If he couldn't find Zulpich this would be as good a target as any, especially as dusk was getting closer. His bombs would have to go soon, otherwise he would be forced to take them back to base and he'd feel a fool if he had to do that.

The flight leader's plane began to lose height. The town loomed up bigger and bigger. He could see the onion-towered church quite plainly now. Hastily his eyes swept the valley from left to right. No sign of flak. The town seemed to be undefended. He came still lower to come in for his bombing run. They swooped in at three hundred miles an hour. Suddenly the intercom was full of the bombardier's triumphant cry: 'BOMBS

AWAY!' The plane lurched abruptly and rose in the air as the thirteen 250 lb general purpose bombs were released. Down below pillars of smoke started to rise to the sky. The other five planes followed their leader and released their bombs. He watched their efforts attentively and noted approvingly that they were all on target. The six B-29s left the scene of destruction and zoomed away to the horizon, hurrying home to debriefing and bacon and eggs. Down below the smoke thickened and rose higher.

In Malmédy the surprised men of the 30th Division and the remaining Belgian civilians had no idea what had hit them. They had looked up at the bright dots in the sky with interest but without fear. No warning had sounded, and one or two of the soldiers had said reassuringly that they were 'ours'. Then the bombs had come raining down. The centre of the town disappeared in a cloud of roaring smoke. When it was over and the men of the 322nd Bombardment Group had departed, thirty-nine miles away from their target of Lammersum, the survivors crawled out of the wreckage and began to count their losses.

At once the telephone began to ring at the headquarters of the Commanding General of the 30th Division. Moments later General Hobbs was talking to an Air Force General in Luxemburg. It wasn't the first time that the 30th Division had been bombed by the Ninth Air Force. Some cynics in the Division were already dubbing them the Ninth *The American Luftwaffe*. At least thirty-seven men of the 120th Infantry had been killed and a large number wounded. An unknown number of civilians had also been slaughtered and with the town on fire, it had only been with difficulty that the American commandant had been able to halt a mass flight on to the roads vitally needed by the units attacking Peiper at La Gleize.

The worried Air Corps General, already mentally considering who would be taking the responsibility for the mistake, stammered, 'It can't happen again'. He was badly wrong.[1]

---

[1] Malmédy was bombed again on the following day and yet again on 25 December. The IX Bombardment Division acknowledged its errors, but General Spaatz of US Strategic Air Forces in Europe refused to do so and referred to the 'alleged errors' at Malmédy.

In spite of Harrison's failure to take La Gleize, his sector was the only bright spot in Ridgway's 40-mile line that day and the airborne commander wanted to see what was going on there. Some time just before dusk he appeared at the Château which housed Harrison's CP, the grenades attached to his webbing and ever-present Springfield in his right hand. Harrison got down to briefing the Corps Commander at once, pulling no punches, giving him the situation as it was without the frills.

'Our attacks from the west and east bogged down today,' he said, 'But tomorrow I'm going to try one from the north.' He beckoned the Corps Commander to the wall map and showed him the situation and then indicated his own approach for the morrow. Ridgway listened carefully. He knew that there was an embarrassment to Harrison's plan—the Combat Command B of the 3rd Armored. The rest of that division was being hard pressed by the German advance and its commander, General Maurice Rose, was crying out for the return of his men. Yet Hobbs would counter that if the CCB was taken away from him, La Gleize would be open from two sides and it would be impossible to mop up the bridgehead force. Peiper might even be able to escape from the trap that had been built up around him at such a price over the last two days. So Ridgway did not tell Harrison these problems. He decided to let him get on with it and to solve the problem of the 3rd's missing combat command when he got back to his own CP.

2

The 155 mm was shaking Peiper more than any other gun he had ever run into. It seemed to shake his very innards to pieces every time it fired. Many of his men were in a constant state of shock from the terrible pounding they were having to endure. Peiper knew they couldn't last very much longer. But still headquarters had not sent him the order to withdraw that he must have if he were to save what was left of his battered command.

During the night the Luftwaffe had tried to drop fuel and ammunition to him, but his supply officer estimated that they had received only ten per cent of the drop at the most. Thus, when the signalmen called him to the radio truck to receive a message from the divisional commander, he ran across and grabbed the earphones eagerly. It might be the order he was so impatiently waiting for—but it wasn't.

At the other end, clouded in static, the strangely impersonal voice, said: 'If *Kampfgruppe* Peiper does not report its supply situation punctually, it cannot reckon on a running supply of fuel and ammunition. Six Royal Tigers ready for action east of Stavelot. Where do you want us to send them?'

Peiper flushed with rage at the unrealistic demands of his commander, who hadn't the slightest idea what a mess he was in, trapped in this miserable little Belgian village. 'Send via air lift to La Gleize,' he forced himself to say through clenched teeth.

Then he pulled himself together. 'We must be allowed to break out immediately.'

At the other end, there was silence, then his commander asked: 'Can you break out with all vehicles and wounded?'

Peiper felt his heart leap. This was the first time that higher headquarters had even remotely considered the possibility. He wasn't going to be abandoned after all.

Urgently he pressed the catch and spoke, just as another shell came crashing down making the ground tremble below his feet. 'Last chance to break out tonight . . . Without wounded and vehicles . . . Please give permission.'

His commander did not give him a straight answer, but promised he would take the matter up with Corps. Peiper signed off and ran for the shelter of his CP. He was confident now that he'd get permission to withdraw and there was no time to be lost. He must get his officers together and plan a route.

There were no protests when he told the news to his commanders that they were going to break out of La Gleize. They knew that they had lost the battle, and that no good purpose would now be served by their sacrificing their lives in the village. Most of them had a pretty shrewd idea by this time that the advance was stymied and the rest of the division would not be able to break through to them. They had to think of their men now and get as many out as possible. Of course the operation would be risky, but it would be better than just waiting for death in La Gleize with that damned cannon shaking them to pieces.

Quickly they circled the map while Peiper sketched in their position as far as he knew it. They were, all of them realised, surrounded, with their own nearest units somewhere on the other side of the Amblève near Stavelot. However, the countryside was rugged and heavily wooded and favoured the escape of even such a large group as their own. Peiper poked his finger at the little dirt road that led down the hill past the priest's house. That's the road they would take.

Abandoning their vehicles, leaving them to be blown by a small band of volunteers after the main group had gone, they would proceed down the narrow road on foot, following it down into the valley towards the hamlet of La Venne, which was still not in American hands. From thence they would have to reconnoitre a route to the Amblève—perhaps to the south of Trois Ponts, where they might be able to cross unobserved.

He finished his briefing and waited for their questions. There was only one of any importance. It was '*When?*' 'Tomorrow morning between two and three,' he answered.

Leaving his officers to work out the details for their own sections, or what was left of them, he called McCown to his CP. 'We've been called back,' he told his prisoner, trying to hide the desperation of his position with the phrase.

Major McCown smiled wearily, realising that this meant long months in a POW cage somewhere in Germany for him. Then remembering how in the course of their long conversation in the cellar on the night of the first day, Peiper had sworn he would ride a Royal Tiger one day, McCown quipped, 'Well, I've always wanted to ride on a Royal Tiger.'

Peiper forced a smile, but did not tell his captive that they would be walking out of La Gleize. Then he got down to business. 'My immediate concern is what to do with the American prisoners and my own wounded.' He explained he would make a deal with the American. If he agreed to release all his American prisoners, except for McCown who was to be kept as a hostage, would the latter guarantee that whoever the American commander was who took La Gleize would release all the German wounded? He would leave one of his own men with the wounded to take care of them. Once they had been released, he would send McCown back to his own lines.

The return of the prisoners was an important principle for Peiper. He knew he could not break out successfully if he were burdened by seriously wounded men. But the *Leibstandarte* had always prided itself on never leaving prisoners in enemy hands if possible. The campaign in Russia had taught the division that very unpleasant things happened to prisoners who belonged to an outfit which bore the name 'Adolf Hitler'.

McCown shook his head. 'Colonel, that proposal is a farce. For one thing I have no power to bind the American command regarding German POWs. After all, you're not in a very good bargaining position.'

'I know,' Peiper replied. 'But I'd like to go ahead with the plan in the hope that your commander will agree.'

McCown considered for a moment. Outside, the ground shook again as another 155 mm shell landed. 'All I can do is sign a statement that I heard you make this offer. I can't do anything more.'

Peiper replied that that would suit him and another captured American was brought in, Captain Bruce Crisinger, ex-commander of Company A, 823rd TD Battalion. The two men, signed the statement that McCown drew up in English and it was handed to the captain, who was to remain with the 150-odd Americans then in Peiper's hands.

It was 1700 exactly when Peiper was called out to the radio car. It was already dark and the frost was beginning to sparkle on the metal sides of the tanks. The American bombardment was starting to ease up a little, but it still did not pay to hang around the littered, shell-holed street for too long. The big American gun over the other side of the ridge at the Château du Froide Cour was still pounding away with frightening regularity. He hurried across to the truck. His young radio officer was crouched over the set, his usual calm 'communications voice' nervous and high. 'Where main line of resistance?' he was asking over and over again. 'Where covering positions? May we break out? *I repeat, may we break out?*'

The receiver began to crackle and Peiper leaned over the man's shoulder impatiently. This *must* be it!

Distorted by static the voice at the other end said: 'State when and where you will cross our lines?'

Peiper's tired face cracked into a smile. The radio officer looked up at him, almost in triumph, as if they had achieved a kind of victory.

But the message was not yet finished. The strangely inanimate voice continued: 'You may break out but only if you bring all wounded and vehicles.'

Peiper's temper snapped. His face flushed angrily. 'Blow the damn thing up!' he roared to the radio officer. 'Permission or not, we're breaking out of here on foot!'

3

Far to Peiper's rear a crisis was developing between the American commanders and the British general whose appointment to the command of two American armies had been indirectly brought about by Peiper's drive west. On the 22nd, Montgomery had saved the 7th Armored Division from being virtually wiped out at the surrounded town of St Vith by insisting, despite the protests of General Ridgway, that it should withdraw in time before the Germans overwhelmed it. No sooner had he solved that crisis than a new and more serious one arose. Early on the morning of the 23rd Montgomery had suggested that the grossly overextended 82nd Airborne should be withdrawn to the almost impregnable ridge south of Werbomont, which provided an ideal defensive position.

Immediately there was a cry of protest from the airborne commanders, used to fighting out on a limb and being cut off from their rear. From General Gavin, concerned with the reputation of his unit, the reaction was that his division had never retreated in 'its combat history' and it wasn't going to start now. Ridgway supported the outspoken Gavin; he could never understand the infantryman's concern for his flanks anyway. Hodges hesitated. He was in a very difficult position. He knew that Bradley had regarded him and his First Army as tempermental throughout the campaign. Now, well aware of Bradley's touchy nature when his personal prestige was questioned, he realised that his serving under the Britisher would not help his relationship with his Army Group Commander one bit. In fact, he would soon receive a very direct letter from Bradley warning him that he would tolerate no further withdrawals on the 1st Army front. The writing was on the wall; but still he was under Montgomery's command and not Bradley's. Thus on the 23rd Hodges hesitated.

Montgomery, for his part, could not begin to understand the airborne commanders' violent reaction or Hodges' hesitation. Although he belonged to an army that was steeped in centuries of tradition, the proposed withdrawals were nothing to do with military prestige for him; they were simply tactical manoeuvres. But Montgomery, closed in the self-imposed capsule of almost monastic isolation in his small tactical HQ, surrounded by his handful of 'young men', had no understanding of the feelings of commanders like Gavin or Ridgway.

Both Ridgway and Montgomery had considerable soldierly virtues, but somewhere or other part of their growing-up had been stunted in childhood so that they seemed cut off from the world of their fellows in many ways. The British general had retained an unworldly childlike naivety which made him strangely innocent to the atmosphere around him, allowing him to see only his side of any problem or argument. Ridgway, for his part, had grown up to be overly aggressive in word and deed, as if any sign of weakness would be regarded as a slur on his red-blooded American manhood.

And in these characteristics both men represented the general officer corps of the two armies from which they came. Unlike General Eisenhower, who was a new type of soldier, the manager in uniform so typical of the post-war armies, these officers had struggled through decades of boring, dreary garrison duty, the pariahs of their society in peacetime, carefully hidden away in remote areas where they could do no damage to the 'real' civilian life around them. Now with the war they were experiencing one brief glorious period of existence when they commanded millions of men, and ministers and industrialists hung on their very words.

Thus it was that they had become very jealous of their national military prestige. The British thought they were the *real* soldiers. After all they had had five years of fighting 'Huns', as they called the Germans. It was only natural they should lead and the Americans follow. The American generals, of course, thought differently. They were the ones who were supplying the bulk of the troops and supplies and they were, in fact, 'bailing the British out', as they were wont to say. The Americans felt their apprenticeship was over; they were now going to lead.

For six months since the D-Day landings the underlying conflict between the British and Americans generals smouldered, broke out, in spite of all General Eisenhower's efforts to pacify and appease the two sides, and was put down again. Now, with the appointment of Montgomery to the command of two huge American armies, that underlying conflict came once more to the surface, this time never to be repressed until the war ended and left the wound unhealed. The attempt to get Ridgway to order a withdrawal was the first step in that path which led to Montgomery's disastrous speech of 7 January, 1945 which caused the final break with General Bradley[1]. In embattled La Gleize Colonel Jochen Peiper little realised what lasting effects on the relationship between the two Allies his attack would have.

On that same day, while Montgomery was trying to urge the American airborne commanders to withdraw, another Englishman was causing trouble for the American allies. Peter Lawless, the *Daily Telegraph*'s correspondent to the First Army, was listening attentively to the First Army's spokesman reading out the daily communiqué and his anger was growing steadily as the major's voice droned on. Among the fifty-odd correspondents in the room, he was the only one who knew the truth of what had happened at Malmédy that day when the B-26s of the 322nd Bombardment Group, whose secondary target had been La Gleize, had dropped their bombs. He had seen the burning centre of the town. Now the 1st Army spokesman was trying to do a typical military whitewash job on the incident.

The Major had just said, 'The Germans having entered Malmédy our air force bombed the town,' when Lawless, whose temper lived up to his name, shouted out, 'There were no Germans at Malmédy, you have been bombing your own troops and have killed three hundred Americans'.[2] There followed an angry scene, but the First Army communiqué remained intact. In the end Peter Lawless stomped out angrily,

---

[1] On that date Montgomery 'explained' the battle to the Press. As Bradley and many other American generals interpreted the speech, it looked as if Montgomery had rescued the American troops who had been caught with their pants down due to the carelessness of 12th Army Group. Bradley never forgave Montgomery and told Eisenhower he would rather resign than serve under him again. Patton sided with Bradley, and Eisenhower was forced at last to come down on the U.S. side. After that his strategic decisions were made strictly from a nationalistic point of view.

[2] No official figures have ever been issued for the casualties incurred in the three-day bombing of Malmédy. Nor has any convincing explanation ever been given for the reason why the Ninth Air Force continued to bomb Malmédy. Some Belgian sources maintain that as the Americans suspected that there were Germans in Malmédy—presumably Skorzeny's men disguised in US uniform—they preferred to blast the town and its US defenders rather than risk this vital bastion falling into German hands.

looking for a stiff drink.[1] Even in defeat Peiper was indirectly causing trouble all along the Allied line.

But long-range trouble was also being prepared for Jochen Peiper. For the first time one of his senior officers had been captured. Late on the evening of 22 December the greater part of Captain Koblenz's reconnaissance company, belonging to Knittel's Reconnaissance Battalion which had attacked along the road to Trois Ponts, was captured, including Captain Koblenz himself.

Already the American command was becoming aware of the killings that had taken place in the Amblève valley. On the 20th, soldiers of the 117th Infantry, clearing the villages of Parfondruy and Ster, had counted the corpses of 117 men, women and children killed by small arms fire.[2] When the local police chief had shown the soldiers the bodies, they had found it difficult to restrain themselves and when nine prisoners were taken from Knittel's battalion, Captain John Kent of Company A had to intervene to prevent his men from killing them.

Thus when Captain Koblenz was captured he was interrogated at once by German-speaking Captain Kurth. That interrogation was followed by individual cross-examination of his men. It took all day, but when it was finished on the 23rd, Captain Koblenz counter-signed each 'statement' made by his men. These statements were forwarded to Major Moore, who belonged to the Inspector General's Office of the 1st Army. From there these first pieces of written evidence slowly moved up the chain of command until they reached Versailles where the clerks filed them away carefully against the day when they would be used in the attempt to hang *one Joachim or Jochen Peiper—SS officer in the Adolf Hitler Division.*

[1] Lawless did not survive the war. He was killed at Remagen.
[2] Naturally the fact that these civilians were found killed by small arms fire does not prove that they were all, or even in great part, deliberately killed by the Germans.

Day Nine:

SUNDAY, 24 DECEMBER, 1944

'We are going to lick the Germans here today!'
General Ridgway, Order of the Day,
24 December, 1944.

It was between two and three in the morning when the surviving SS men started to slip out of La Gleize and make their way in little groups down the steep slope that led out of the village in the general direction of the River Amblève. There were only eight hundred left out of the 5,000 who had set off a week before. Peiper knew that he was finally beaten, that the whole counter-offensive had failed. There would be no drive to the Meuse now, no capture of Antwerp, no major victory with the British and American armies divided, no radical change in the future course of the war.

Later, after he was captured, he would have time, thirteen years indeed, to consider where he had gone wrong. Over and over again he would ask himself why he had forgotten to have engineers well up in front of the column when he had been stopped by mines outside Lanzerath on that first day. He would torture himself trying to find an explanation for his failure to take Stavelot on the night of the 17th when it lay wide open for the taking. Why had he overlooked the vital necessity of having a bridging unit with each armoured point? How much time had he lost when the bridges across the Amblève and Salm were blown in front of his nose on the 18th and 19th? The advance of his *Kampfgruppe* through the Ardennes was, he knew, one of the boldest actions of his whole career (a fact to which Allied military thinkers would testify when the hatred and partisan passions of war had died down); yet he had made mistakes—too many mistakes.

But as he led his men down the road from La Gleize Peiper had little time for self-recriminations. Somehow or other he must have his men well away from La Gleize before the *Amis* discovered that the birds had flown. The column stumbled on through the knee-deep snow, the one American prisoner guarded by young Paul Froehlich, who somehow managed to keep his pistol levelled at McCown the whole time.

Two hours had passed since the column had sneaked out of La Gleize. The village lay in silence. Down in the cellars around the ruined church the American prisoners still slept, guarded by the few SS men who had stayed behind to cover the withdrawal.

With a great roar the first charge exploded. In the cellars the prisoners started out of their sleep, faces taut with shock. Another explosion rocked the village. Outside tank after tank, left behind by the *Kampfgruppe*, went up in flames. The last defenders of La Gleize, fifty in all, were destroying the heavy equipment of their once-proud regiment. The night was shattered by the explosions, and flames shot into the air on all sides. The whole of La Gleize and the surrounding countryside seemed to be burning.

Down below in the circle of hills that surrounded the village, the weary Americans, who were trying to grab a few hours sleep before the morning attack, flung themselves out of their bedrolls and ran for the snow-filled foxholes.

In his château headquarters just beyond La Gleize, General Harrison woke with a start and groaned when he heard the noise. With both Hodges and Ridgway crying out that he should take La Gleize so that the latter could have Boudinot's armour to bolster up the sagging XVIII Corps line, what new trick had the enemy found to foil his attack of the morrow? Would La Gleize never fall?

McCown plodded on through the snow at the side of the young German commander. The pace was murderous. They had been going all night, stopping every hour for a brief five minutes rest. Then the seemingly inexhaustible Peiper would come round checking each man solicitously, encouraging them to keep up and laughing at any sign of weakness. In spite of the fact that Peiper represented everything that McCown had been taught to hate, he could not but admire him; he was a damn good soldier and a born leader, whose men admired him totally.

Dawn came and still they marched on. McCown wondered what was happening to the rest of the prisoners from the 111th Battalion whom they had left behind at La Gleize. In spite of his aching leg muscles and snow-blinded eyes, he smiled a little wryly to himself. They would be celebrating Christmas tomorrow with their own buddies. Perhaps they'd even have turkey and all the trimmings. After what they had been through, the authorities would probably make some special provision for them—forty-eight hours leave in Paris or something like that. And what would Christmas Day, 1944, bring for him? The POW cage more likely than not, with a hunk of black bread and a piece of ersatz *wurst* as the highpoint of the day.

His face must have revealed his gloomy train of thought, for Peiper, marching close by, suddenly turned to him and, pointing to a snow-covered fir tree, brilliantly lit by the reflection of the sun, said cheerfully, 'I promised you the other night I would get you a tree for Christmas. Well, there it is!'

Some time later McCown caught up with Peiper again and, pointing to the ever-present Froehlich with his levelled pistol, said, 'Can't you tell this guy to stop calling me "boy?" I am a major, after all' Peiper forced a smile. 'It's the only English he knows,' he explained. Then he turned to the soldier and told him what McCown had said. The latter nodded his understanding. 'Colonel,' he remarked, 'can't you get the Major to give you his word of honour he won't escape. I'm sick of holding this pistol up like this!'

Peiper translated the man's words and in the end McCown gave in. 'All right,' he said, beat and weary, 'I'll give you my word.'

With a grin Froehlich put away his pistol.

Just after eight o'clock on the morning of the 24th, Peiper told his men they could rest again. They flopped into the snow and, without even bothering to take cover, stretched out in exhaustion. Suddenly their rest was disturbed by the sound of artillery fire from the direction of La Gleize. They sat up abruptly. Shells were landing on La Gleize again, on the other side of the valley from where they now lay. They could see tiny figures advancing on the empty village from all sides. McCown, who had bound a white handkerchief round his helmet,[1] so that Peiper thought he looked like 'an umpire at a tactical exercise', said sadly: 'Poor general, they'll fire him for sure for this one.' Then the firing stopped as the *Amis* discovered that the birds had already flown.

The exhausted men laughed as they thought of the surprised looks on the faces of the *Amis* when they discovered that the village was empty.

Peiper laughed too, but in spite of his pleasure at the final trick he had pulled on the Americans, which confirmed his opinion that they weren't much good as soldiers, he knew that his situation was still exceedingly dangerous. He wasn't out of the mess yet. Nor was he happy about the attitude of his men; they were smoking, careless of the danger, and during the march, his NCOs had been forced to use clubs to keep them from sinking into the snow and going off to sleep. 'All right,' he ordered, 'on your feet; let's go!'

A little while later Peiper quickened his pace and, with a few of his staff, soon left the rest of the column behind. Major McCown watched him go, his figure getting smaller and smaller by the minute until finally he disappeared into a clump of firs. McCown did not know it, but he wasn't to see the

[1] Presumably to make himself known as a POW.

German again for nearly two years and when he did, their roles would be reversed.

The artillery bombardment had stopped now. Task Force Harrison advanced cautiously into La Gleize, for which it had fought so desperately these last few days, to find it empty save for a few SS men who had covered the withdrawal and had volunteered to stay behind and blow up the tanks. Most of them surrendered without a fight. Private Hall, who had been captured at Stoumont a couple of days before, remembers his guard simply putting down his rifle and raising his dirty hands wordlessly.

The tired dispirited infantrymen who had believed they were fated never to break the stubborn SS defence of the village moved freely through the two cobbled streets, littered with the debris of war and holed with the giant craters made by the 155 mm guns. They stared down at the German wounded, especially at young First Lieutenant Venoni Junker, who had a great cavity in his chest and Peiper's own Iron Cross pinned to his tunic (it had been one of Peiper's last acts before he left La Gleize). The cross went, as did most of the other decorations the GIs could get their hands on. Joined by the happy, newly-liberated prisoners, freed from the nightmare possibility of a German POW cage for the rest of the war, they stared round-eyed at their booty. It was considerable, the most any outfit had netted till then. Twenty-eight tanks, seventy half-tracks and twenty-five artillery pieces in the place itself with more in the surrounding countryside. Tired as they were, the infantrymen, who had expected that morning to meet fanatical SS men, prepared to die in a last-ditch stand, were relaxed and noisy, shouting at each other happily, clambering on the captured vehicles, heedless of booby-traps like a group of excited schoolboys suddenly released from the confines of school.[1]

---

[1] Naturally most of the German equipment was damaged or destroyed. Only the vehicles and guns close to the houses occupied by the Americans or German wounded were not blown up by the rearguard party.

Many of these men would not survive the next six months, but on that day they knew, even the weariest of them, that they had achieved a victory—a greater one than most of them were ever to realise. They had broken the spearhead of the élite German Sixth SS Panzer Army, and with it Adolf Hitler's premier division, which no longer could be considered an armoured formation in any sense of the word. Within a matter of hours they and the rest of the US Thirtieth Infantry Division would be holding an unbroken line north of the River Amblève all the way from Malmédy to Stoumont. The first and most crucial phase of the Battle of the Bulge was over and the Americans had won it.

2

Early that Christmas Eve there were plenty of staff officers in the Allied camp who were not aware of the victory. Indeed, Christmas Eve in the far western sector of the Bulge found uneasiness in virtually every American headquarters from the individual front-line battalions right up to the rear-line headquarters of the First Army itself. The attack Montgomery had planned for the VII Corps had turned out to be a purely defensive battle. To the east the 3rd Armored Division, which Ridgway urgently needed to bolster up his over-extended XVIII Airborne Corps, was being subjected to heavy pressure, with some of its troops actually surrounded by the Germans. It was under these circumstances that Montgomery finally managed to convince Ridgway that his corps had to be 'tidied up' immediately if he did not want to be faced with disaster. On the morning of the 24th he had arrived at Ridgway's farmhouse headquarters outside Werbomont in an open touring car without escort, unlike the unfortunate Supreme Commander who was still being held prisoner in his Versailles headquarters. Chirpy and yet cautious, he put Ridgway in the picture.

As he saw it, the fall of St Vith the previous day meant that the Germans would exert fresh pressure with the forces now released from the St Vith battle and that German reinforcements would begin to flow through the newly captured road and rail centre. This pressure would be felt towards the centre and right of Ridgway's line. In the main it would hit the bulge occasioned by the deployment of Gavin's 82nd Airborne. Ridgway said nothing, but waited for what he knew must come. Montgomery did not hesitate. The 82nd would have to be evacuated to a sensible defence line, probably the road running from Trois Ponts to Manhay.

Ridgway's reaction was cold. A disciple of constant attack, Montgomery's proposal was anathema to him; but Montgomery was his boss, he had made up his mind and he would not change it. The two generals shook hands and Montgomery left, waving happily to the G.I. sentries, before he set off to drive to General Hodges' HQ to tell him what he had ordered the American First Army Commander's men to do.

Some time later Ridgway called his divisional commanders for a conference at his HQ. He laid it on the line to them without any preliminaries. 'Starting after dark,' he said. 'Combat Command A of the Seventh Armored will withdraw to Manhay, and the 82nd Airborne to Trois Ponts.'

Hasbrouck of the 7th Armored and Hoge of the 9th Armored nodded their approval, but Gavin protested sharply. As he wrote after the war, '[he was] greatly concerned with the attitude of the troops . . . the Division never having made a withdrawal in its combat history'.

In his heart Ridgway agreed with Gavin but he had his orders to carry out and carry them out he would. Nevertheless Gavin's words had unsettled him. Unlike Montgomery he could not view the withdrawal clinically as a purely tactical measure. For him questions of morale and prestige were involved. He decided that the troops must be told that once they had carried out the withdrawal they would retreat no more, but stand and fight where they were.

Swiftly he composed the order of the day, ending it with the words:

In my opinion this is the dying gasp of the German Army. He is putting everything he has into this fight. We are going to smash that final drive here today in this Corps zone. This command is the command that will smash the German offensive spirit for this war. Impress every man in your division with that spirit. We are going to lick the Germans here today.

The decision to withdraw was the saving of the last survivors of *Kampfgruppe* Peiper. By the time night fell, they had covered over twenty miles; food was limited to a handful of hard biscuits, swallowed with a couple of shots of cognac. McCown was finding the going increasingly tough; he had little control over his limbs and his legs felt like jelly. Once Peiper's regimental surgeon had given him a piece of candy and for a time the sugar had given him renewed energy. Now the new commander of the main body forced the pace, marching them on without a break, as if he knew that the river and freedom were within sight. Occasionally a man dropped in the snow, but the young captain who led them, would tolerate no drop-outs. 'If you fall behind, you'll be shot!' he cried and made a threatening gesture towards his holster; the man would stagger to his feet and carry on.

Soon after nightfall they crossed the Amblève by a small wooden bridge, and found themselves in a thickly wooded area through which the 82nd Airborne was withdrawing. The exhausted SS men, who had earlier passed within yards of American positions without being detected, now kept bumping into the paratroopers and skirmishes were developing on all sides. In the confused fighting in the dark, the Germans suffered their first casualties of the withdrawal, but the young captain was determined not to abandon his wounded once again. Anyone who was hit, had his equipment stripped from him, was hauled to his feet and dragged on by his comrades. Escape was within sight; the Salm had been located and a crossing point as yet unoccupied by the retreating *Amis*, had been found. Time was now of the essence.

Major McCown was at the end of his strength. He knew that he could not take the pace much longer. All he wanted to do was to drop down in the snow and rest. Suddenly artillery fire erupted into the night. Red flames leapt up in the trees a couple of hundred yards to the south in front of the SS column. The young captain ordered his men to halt, surprised at the direction of the bombardment and not realising that it came from the 82nd withdrawing towards them. But they didn't stop for long. Tracer bullets started to cut the air close by, followed by the chatter of an American machine-gun. The SS men scattered. The firing seemed to be coming from all sides.

McCown dropped into the snow and kept his head down. Mortar bombs began to fall all around him. He raised his head cautiously. Froehlich, his guard, was nowhere to be seen. From all sides came confused commands in German and English. Somewhere close by, there were American troops. This might be his last chance! Carefully he levered himself up and began to crawl in the direction of the American fire. Bullets cut the air all about him. Someone yelled something in German. If it was Froehlich, he would have to come and find him. After a hundred yards of crawling, the front of his body soaked by the snow, his face torn and ripped by the firs, he stood up. Swallowing hard and trying to wet his cracked lips, he began to whistle. Whistling as loud as he could, he struck out towards the sound of the firing. After what seemed like an age he heard a voice shout out, 'Halt, Goddammit!' He knew he had made it.

Moments later, helping hands were guiding him forward through the line of foxholes of Colonel Ekman's 505th Parachute Infantry towards the regimental command post, where Ekman had just received permission to break off the fight with Peiper. The withdrawal was more important; he was to let the German go. But Major McCown was no longer concerned with *Ober-*

sturmbannfuehrer Peiper. He was with his own people again. It was Christmas Day and he was a free man. It was the best Christmas present he had had in his whole life. There is little more to tell. Peiper had reached the safety of his own lines a little before the other survivors of *Kampfgruppe* Peiper who swam the icy, fast-flowing River Salm in the early hours of Christmas morning and made contact with elements of their own division some four miles to the east of the 82nd Airborne. The exhausted, dripping-wet SS men were welcomed back by their comrades like victors instead of the remnants of a defeated formation. One day later they were transferred to the near St Vith to recuperate. But the decimated 1st SS Panzer Regiment, the élite of the élite, would not fight again in the Ardennes battle. Although two ordnance companies went to work to rearm them, all that the 1st SS Panzer Regiment could muster was one lone tank company.

That Christmas Day, while the survivors sank into an exhausted sleep, oblivious of the war still raging all around them, the men of the 30th Division's 117th and 120th Infantry Regiments began the slow work of beating the woods around La Gleize for survivors. There were rumours of 25 tanks hiding out in the road cuts north of Trois Ponts, but they proved unfounded. The last tank left operational on the American side of the River Amblève was a Royal Tiger that had been disabled outside the burned-out Antoine Farm which had once served as Major Knittel's headquarters. Captain Goltz ordered his few remaining men to withdraw over the river and then when they were safely across he set fire to the seventy-two ton monster. When he was satisfied that the fire could not be put out, he left. The last of Peiper's men on the western bank of the Amblève had gone.

Epilogue

Throughout the last spring of the war the Judge Advocate's branch of the United States Army had been assiduously collecting evidence against Jochen Peiper's *Kampfgruppe*. Those men of the *Leibstandarte* who had been captured in Belgium were segregated in a special camp in France and repeatedly cross-examined as to the names of the men who had been with Peiper on that fateful drive into the Ardennes. McCown was asked to prepare a report for Intelligence on his experiences when he was Peiper's prisoner, while in Brussels the Prince Regent of Belgium ordered a special committee, made up of lawyers and university teachers, to investigate the alleged shootings of civilians in the Amblève valley, and in particular, in the Trois Ponts–Stavelot area. By April, 1945, it had finished its investigation. Bit by bit a case was being built up against Colonel Peiper and the surviving eight hundred men of his group who had fled that night from La Gleize and reached the safety of their own lines on Christmas Day.

Then the war ended. It found the *Leibstandarte* in Austria, grouped around the area of Vienna. As assistant divisional commander Peiper marched into captivity with the rest of his once-proud formation, blinded by that particularly German romantic notion that now the fighting had stopped the peace could start with as little unpleasantness as possible. But the young assistant divisional commander was in for a rude shock. The end of the second World War was not like a 19th century historical novel with dignified ex-enemies congratulating each other, handing over swords with mumbled embarrassed comments of 'hard luck' and going their way with shoulders squared in gallant adversity. The bitter reality of that first summer of peace was brutally different. The price of defeat would now have to be paid.

Soon names such as Belsen and Buchenwald began to loom large on the horizon. The newspapers were full of photographs of Germans such as Ilse Koch and Josef Kramer. There was talk of lampshades made of human skin, soap out of human fat, sadistic orgies in which the slave victims died when they had satisfied their jackbooted masters' perverted sexual passions. The statistics began to flood the headlines—one million Poles killed, six million Jews, perhaps twelve million Russians.

That summer the victors wanted to punish the perpetrators. The culprits would have to pay. The rules pertaining to the punishment of murder were applied by the Americans to war. Every war, their reasoning went, is a kind of murder. If my opponent has unleashed that war, then he is a murderer and I have the right to punish him for it. In the United States in particular, an attempt was made to establish the impossible: to place war on a legal footing and to apply civilian peacetime rules to it.

But there were still eighty million Germans. Were they all guilty? How did one identify the culprit? The victors saw the criminal most in the person of the SS man. His cap bore a silver 'death's head', symbol of the murderer.

For the average man in the street in the countries which had fought the Germans, the SS man was the public symbol of that cruel complex of brutal power which had held Europe under its sway. No one stopped to ask whether the SS man was some forty-year-old Herr Doktor who had been in the Party since the beginning and had served as a medical experimenter far behind the front in the sadistic safety of the camps, or some seventeen-year-old conscript who had been forced into the *Waffen SS* to fight in some desperate, last-ditch battle.

By the beginning of December, 1945, some eleven hundred members of the *Leibstandarte* had been questioned and the number who were to be retained for further cross-examination reduced to about four hundred. These were transported from their various camps to Schwäbisch-Hall in the first week of that month where the number of the accused was further reduced to seventy-four. The preparations for the Malmédy trial were entering their final stage.

It seemed fitting to the Allied War Crimes Commission that the seventy-four accused of the *Leibstandarte Adolf Hitler* should be tried in that little town outside of Munich, which symbolised for many millions of non-Germans the epitome of Nazi horror—Dachau. By May, 1946, the dreary one-storey brown wooden huts were ready for the 'Malmédy Men'. While the carpenters still hammered in the main court and the electricians rigged up the lines for the pressmen's telephones and the newsreels' lights, the SS men were brought from Schwäbisch-Hall and housed in the cell block of the camp's bunker. Close by, the fifty-four of their ex-comrades who would testify against them were accommodated in Cage III, Block 202, while the Belgian civilian witnesses were given the luxury of a separate villa.

Among the accused were Generals Dietrich, Kraemer and Priess, Peiper and all his surviving company commanders, many of his senior NCOs, including Siptrott, Ochmann, his driver Zwigart, and a whole group of private soldiers who had 'confessed' at Schwäbisch-Hall, including one who had been sixteen at the time of the Ardennes Offensive.

The Prosecution consisted of the same team that had cross-examined them at Schwäbisch-Hall and elsewhere—Perl, Thon, Fenton and the rest of the War Crimes Team, under the command of Lt-Colonel Ellis. In the main the case rested on the statements obtained in Schwäbisch-Hall, but Ellis was to call the surviving American witnesses of the shooting at the Baugnez corner and a few of the Belgians, such as Peter Rupp, Mme Gregoire, Mlle Lochner, who one day would become Mme Tombeaux as a result of the friendship she formed during the trial with another civilian witness M. Tombeaux, who had escaped from the shootings at Parfondruy—perhaps the only happy thing to emerge from the Dachau trial.

To defend them, the accused had seven German civilian lawyers, hastily appointed before the start of the trial from jurists who, in this year of the great de-Nazification cases when so many of their colleagues had lost their right to practice because of their Nazi associations, wanted little to do with the 'SS criminals', as the Malmédy men were beginning to be called in the German press. In addition, an American defender was appointed, a slim Army lawyer from Atlanta, Georgia, Lt-Colonel Willis M. Everett Jr who held the official title of Chief Defence Counsel. We do not know now why he took on the job (he is long since dead and he left his motives unrecorded), but it was a hard decision to make that spring of 1946, especially when his 'clients' looked on him with undisguised scorn as an American concession to democracy, who would merely go through the motions of defending them. They were to be surprised.

The Dachau trial opened on 16 May. Everywhere tall MPs in their best uniforms guarded doors and windows. They sprang to attention when Brigadier-General Dalbey, the President of the Court, entered, followed by the panel of seven officers of field grade and Colonel A. H. Rosenfeld, the legal adviser to the Court. Then the prisoners were brought in, led by the Provost Marshal and surrounded by MPs. They were escorted to the pen facing the table for the judges and made to sit down. They were neatly dressed in former Wehrmacht uniforms, devoid of the badges of rank and the medals which had once proudly adorned their chests. Each man bore a large card on his back and front, with a number printed on it in black. Dietrich was eleven, Kraemer thirty-three and Priess forty-five. Peiper was forty-two.

Most of the first morning was spent in reading out the charges. The details went on and on, first in English, then in German. The pedantic bureaucratic words, read in a monotonous voice, revealed nothing of the horror and enormity of the deeds they described; 'beaten over the head with rifle butts', 'lined up against the wall and mown down', 'taken out and shot in the garden one by one'.

Even the prisoners began to fidget on the hard seats and glanced around the court. Peiper, sitting next to his former Corps Commander, Priess, rested his cheek in his hand and stared cynically at the judges and then at the 'defender'. He knew what he could expect from both of them. Only when their individual names were read out did the ex-SS men pay much attention to the court's proceedings.

Thus it went on all morning until, at twelve o'clock precisely, General Dalbey ordered the court recessed. That afternoon the prosecution could begin its case.

Colonel Ellis opened his case with an aggressive attack on the accused. He told the court that 'some of the troops [of the *Leibstandarte*] were told to excel in the killing of prisoners of war as well as in fighting'. 'Others were told to make plenty of *rabbatz*, which in SS parlance means to have plenty of fun killing everything that comes in sight ... Others were told to bump off everything that comes before their guns.' As he read from his brief, it was obvious that he believed everything he told the court, but that he was aware too of the weakness of the 'statements'. He warned his listeners that some of the prosecution witnesses might turn against him. The fact that they were German soldiers might lead them to support the defendants when the time came.

He introduced his case with witnesses from the *Kampfgruppe* who had agreed to testify against their former leaders. Four enlisted men confirmed that Peiper had told them on the eve of the battle 'to drive on recklessly, give no quarter and take no prisoners ... everything that came into our sights should be mown down'. They said they were told to 'remember the women and children killed in the Allied air attacks and take no prisoners'. Corporal Ernst Kohler of the 1st Regiment said his platoon was told 'to avenge the lives of our women and children. Show no mercy to Belgian civilians. Take no prisoners'. Captain Oskar Klingelhoefer and Lts Junker and Heinz Tomhardt agreed with Kohler's statement. Lt Tomhardt said, 'I told my men that they were not permitted to take prisoners. Then I told them that they were not to shoot at prisoners of war who waved their helmets'.[1]   These witnesses were followed by twenty-year-old Corporal Gustav Sprenger who testified that when he went into the little church at La Gleize to aid a wounded German, he saw a hundred American soldiers lined up across the square in the schoolyard. A few moments later he 'heard machine pistol and rifle fire from the direction of the school, a great deal of shooting'. Twenty minutes later when he emerged, 'American soldiers were lying on the ground. Dozens of Americans, shot in sheds, against cemetery walls and wherever else they were captured'. Then Sprenger admitted he had shot a wounded American soldier himself. The man was lying on a stretcher and after two of his comrades had murdered the Americans carrying the stretcher, he shot the man on the ground.

Rapidly Ellis built up his case, basing it on premeditated murder of prisoners and civilians by troops who had been given specific orders to carry out the killings prior to the entry into battle. Calling Dietrich to the witness stand he got him to state that at a conference with the Fuehrer at Bad Nauheim on 11 December, 1944, five days prior to the start of the offensive, the Leader had given out a general order for a campaign of terror. 'The Fuehrer said we would have to act brutally and show no human inhibitions. He also said that a wave of fright and terror should precede the attack and that the enemy resistance was to be broken by terror.' The former commanding general of the Sixth SS Panzer Army was then asked by Ellis about a conference he had held himself a day later, at which he issued his final orders to his divisional commanders. At that conference he had made no mention of collecting points for the expected prisoners of war and one of those present, thinking he had overlooked the provision of POW cages, had asked: 'And the prisoners? Where shall we put them?'

'Prisoners?' Dietrich had replied, 'You know what to do with them?'

Questioned about this 'Pontius Pilate' reply, Dietrich said it meant that the Hague Conventions were to be respected. But no

[1] A recognition signal for German troops disguised as Americans.

one believed him, especially as Peiper confirmed that the terror order had been passed down to the lower echelons, adding that the order stated that the battle should be conducted 'stubbornly, with no regard for Allied prisoners of war, who will have to be shot if the situation makes it necessary and compels it'.

While Ellis piled up the evidence against the SS men, Everett remained silent. Once he asked that the accused should be divided into three groups according to rank—officers, NCOs and enlisted men. He felt that this division might help to strengthen the resistance of the individual groups. But he had no luck with his application. Ellis jumped up and made a melodramatic protest against the change. 'The defendants are together as joint perpetrators of Malmédy and other massacres. Each defendant was a cog in a giant slaughter machine,' he said fervently. 'They are asking for severance simply because the teeth of the machine meshed less smoothly when they were dripping with blood than when they were lubricated with the oil of victory.' It was a florid statement, meaning very little, but at that time and under those circumstances, no one thought to question its logic. Colonel Rosenfeld, who was to become Colonel Everett's bitter enemy during the trial, turned down the application.

Having dealt with the Germans, Ellis turned his attention to those survivors of the 'Massacre' who could still be traced eighteen months after the war had ended. Virgil Lary, as the surviving officer, was naturally a star witness. 'After the first machine-guns fired, men fell dead and wounded all around me,' he told the court. 'The firing lasted about three minutes. A man came by me and I heard a pistol shot nearby. Then I heard the sound of a new clip being inserted in a pistol and the individual passed me . . . I heard someone say to someone else. "Have they killed you yet?" He replied, "No, not yet but if the . . . are going to kill me, I wish they would come back and get it over with".'

Lary paused and looked at the defendants. It was the high-point of his testimony. The Germans, with the number labels around their necks, were only a couple of feet from the witness stand. Lary looked them over carefully and then stretching out a slow hand, he pointed at one of them. 'This is the man who fired two shots into an American prisoner of war,' he said steadily.

Ex-Private Georg Fleps instinctively moved his upper body back as if the hand might strike him.

Samuel Dobyns followed Lary into the witness box. His ambulance had been trapped by German crossfire and he had been forced to surrender. His captors had wanted to shoot him there and then, but an officer had prevented the murder. Later in the field at the crossroads a German had fired a pistol at them and they had broken ranks and tried to run to the rear. Another pistol began to fire and then another. 'At least two machine-guns opened up and we all hit the dirt. I was shot four times and there were eight to ten holes in my jacket. I saw three or four Germans shoot wounded who were crying for help. I thought I was the only one left alive.'

Ex-Military Policeman Homer Ford related how 'Men were lying around moaning and crying. When the Germans came over, they would say, "Is he breathing?" and would either shoot or hit them with the butt of their guns. The closest they came to me was about ten feet. After they fired at us, I lay stretched out with my hands out and I could feel the blood oozing out. I was lying in the snow, and I got wet and started to shiver, and I was afraid they would see me shivering, but they didn't. I had my head down and they couldn't see, but they were walking around the whole bunch and then they went over toward the road junction. I heard them shoot their pistols right next to me. I could hear them pull the trigger back and then the click. The men were moaning and taking on something terrible. I also heard the butt hit the heads and a squishing noise . . . '

Peter Rupp told his story of the happenings in the Hôtel du Moulin and Mme Gregoire what had happened in that Stavelot cellar. Mlle Marette Locher related again how she had peered through the timbers of the cowshed to see Ochmann shoot

Sergeant Abraham Lincoln and the other seven men of his battalion. M. Natalis of Stoumont told of what had happened in the hillside village when the Germans captured it. And with each succeeding testimony it seemed that one more nail had been hammered home finally and irrevocably in the coffin Colonel Burton Ellis was fashioning for the accused men

Gamely Colonel Everett fought back to save his clients. At his own expense he brought Lt-Colonel McCown over from the States to testify on the accused's behalf. The stern-faced colonel made a favourable impression on the court. A little while later he succeeded in getting the ancient *curé* of La Gleize to testify that there had never been a massacre at La Gleize, in fact there had never been a church wall against which the Germans had allegedly placed their victims. The only dead American he, the *curé*, had seen throughout the fighting at La Gleize was one charred body in the turret of a shot-up Sherman. In early June the slim colonel, who eventually was going to spend some forty thousand dollars of his own money to try to save Peiper and his men, notched up another minor victory when one of the officers he had sent out to gather evidence proved that a woman allegedly shot by the SS at Büllingen had actually died the day before when she had been struck by a piece of shrapnel from an *American* shell. But although Everett scored at Ellis's expense because the latter had been so confident of the guilt of the accused that he had failed to prepare his case thoroughly enough, it was obvious that Peiper and his men could not escape.

Just after dawn on 16 July, 1946 Peiper and the prisoners were led into the court house for the last time to hear their sentences. General Dalbey read out the details of the accusation against the ex-colonel; he paused and read out the sentence: 'Death by hanging'.

Tod durch Erhängen, the interpreter said softly, but Peiper knew what the words meant. He licked his lips and said softly '*Danke*'. Turning smartly, he went back the way he had come.

The Malmédy trial was over.

Peiper was never hanged. Nor were any of the defendants. The climate of opinion was changing in Germany. Soon the Germans were no longer enemies or ex-enemies; soon they were potential allies; then they were friends. There was stay-of-execution after stay-of-execution. Peiper and the rest of the high-ranking members of the SS who had been sentenced to death or life-imprisonment at Dachau languished in jail until finally, after thirteen years, he and Dietrich and the other remaining Malmédy defendants were released, on parole at first and then on probation, their movements restricted to the Stuttgart area. The now 43-year-old ex-colonel emerged into a world which was completely alien to him. For a while he took an extended holiday and then he took a job—'got in the steeplechase for money', as he called it contemptuously. But his past continued to haunt him. Upon publication of John Toland's *Battle*, the best-selling American account of the Battle of the Bulge, which appeared in 1959, an Italian recognising his photo in the book accused him of having been connected with a massacre in Northern Italy. Nothing came of the accusation save that Peiper lost his job. It was to be one of many such dismissals.

Today Jochen Peiper is a man approaching sixty. His hair is grey and plastered down in the style of his class in the 30's. There are fine wrinkles around his eyes and his neck is somewhat scrawny and a little too small for his collar. When he reads, he has to use spectacles. But he is still as slim and vital as he was thirty years ago, gesticulating a lot and larding his speech with the tough old *Landserjargon*—soldiers' talk—of the war.

But for all his vitality he is a broken man. 'I am sitting on a powder keg,' he tells you, 'One day someone will come along with another accusation and the powder-keg will explode. Then it'll be all over at last.'

'I'm a fatalist today. The world had branded me and my men as the scum of the earth. And no one will ever be able to clear up the Malmédy mess now. . . Too many lies have been told about that in these last twenty-five years.'

Today there is little visible evidence in the Ardennes of that week in December, 1944, when Peiper's thrust seemed about to take him to the coveted Meuse bridges. There are monuments enough—Büllingen, Baugnez and Ligneuville all have them, dedicated to those young men who came three thousand miles to give their lives so long ago. But naturally there are no monuments to the *1 SS Panzer Division—die Leibstandarte Adolf Hitler*. Yet for the knowledgeable there are still traces to be found of their hectic progress through the fir forests of the Ardennes a quarter of a century ago. Outside the little hamlet of Poteau, for instance, the villagers still show the interested inquirer the deep-ridged furrows across the swampy fields where Peiper's 72-ton Royal Tigers bogged themselves down on the morning of 18 December. At Recht a pasture is still called 'Hanssen's Field' though few of the villagers today know why except an old man who recalls that the 103 members of Hanssen's Panzer Grenadier Regiment, killed in the attempt to force the Amblève Line and relieve their trapped comrades in La Gleize, were buried there.

Thus one can still trace Peiper's route to the Meuse and his particular date with destiny—a series of shallow depressions in the fields around Lodomez where the *Jabos* (fighter-bombers) of the 365th Fighter Group caught Peiper's packed columns—the shattered tree stumps on the heights above Trois Ponts that were cut down by the artillery barrage which stopped Major Knittel's reconnaissance battalion as it turned about and tried to recapture the Stavelot bridge—the waterlogged holes in the forest above Stoumont which had been the American perimeter line, where if you grub around long enough you can find the mouldering 75 mm shell cases with the date '1944' stamped at their base. Or you find a foot-length shaped piece of wood with the shattered bit of rusty metal around its neck that falls to pieces as you touch it; it had once been a German stick grenade.

A trace here, a trace there until you finally drive down the curving road into the dead little village of La Gleize. There, looming up in front of you, is the only surviving tank of the many score with which Jochen Peiper set out so confidently on the morning of 16 December, 1944—a Tiger, as powerful-looking and as sinister as the day it first rumbled so menacingly up the long incline from Trois Ponts down into the green valley below.

Bibliography

Cole, Hugh M. *The Ardennes: The Battle of the Bulge*, Dept. of the Army.
Eisenhower, Dwight D. *Crusade in Europe*, Doubleday & Company.
Eisenhower, John, *The Bitter Woods*, Robert Hale.
Merriam, Robert. *Dark December*, Ziff-Davis.
Montgomery, Bernard: *Memoirs*, World Publishing Co.
Ridgway, Matthew: *Soldier*, Harper and Brothers.
Toland, John: *The Story of the Bulge*, Random House.
Edited: *Kriegsschicksale*, Geschichsverein Zwischen Venn und Schneifel.
Nobecourt, Jacques: *Le dernier Coup de Des d'Hitler*, Laffont.
Giles, J. H. *The G.I. Journal of Sergeant Giles*, Houghton Mifflin Co.
Bovy Marcel: *La Bataille de l'Amblève*, Les Amities Mosanes.
Greil, Lothar: *Die Wahrheit uber Malmédy*, Schild Verlag.
Stein, George: *The Waffen SS*, Cornell University Press.
Kratschmer, E. G. *Die Ritterkreuztrager der Waffen SS*, Plesse Verlag.
Edited: *Crimes de Guerre*, Liège.
Hewitt, R. *Workhorse of the Western Front, 30th Infantry Division*, privately printed.
Calloux, Lucien: *Ardennes 1944 Pearl Harbor en Europe*, privately printed.
United States Senate: *Malmédy Massacre Investigation Hearings 1949*, Govt. Printing office.
Hausser, Paul: *Waffen SS im Einsatz*, Plesse Verlag.
Ziemssen, Dietrich: *Der Malmédy Prozess*, Plesse Verlag.
Potter, Charles: *Days of Shame*, Coward-McCann.

Principal Interviews

Herr Siptrott (Esslingen), Herr Caspari and Herr Hauprich (Wittlich), M. Fagnoul (St Vith), Madame Rupp and M. Lemaire (Ligneuville), M. and Madame Tombeau (Stavelot), M. le Professeur Natalis (Stoumont), Madame Bodarwé and M. Le Joly (Baugnez), M. and Madame Lejeune, M. Pfeiffer (Büllingen), M. Vitz (Honsfeld), M. le Curé Blokiau (La Gleize), Madame Palm (Lanzerath), Herr Jochen Peiper (Stuttgart).

Acknowledgements

In the preparation of this book I owe a great deal to many people. It would be impossible to list all the individuals who helped me. But the following deserve my special thanks: Dr Maurice Delaval of Vielsam, that amateur historian to whom everyone who writes on the Battle of the Bulge must turn at one time or another; Dr. Günther Deschner, Editor-in-Chief, *Sachbuchverlag*, Berthelsmann Inc, Germany, who used his excellent connections on my behalf so often; General Sir Kenneth Strong, Eisenhower's Chief Intelligence Officer during the Battle; John Eisenhower, U.S. Ambassador to Belgium, who, in spite of the heavy duties of his office, found time to advise me on an episode which holds a special place in his heart; M. Kurt Fagnoul of St Vith, Secretary of the local historical society, which does such a wonderful task preserving the heritage of the three former German cantons now part of Belgium; Mr. Calvin Boykin of Texas who sent me a detailed report of his experiences in the first days of the German attack; Tom Stubbs, librarian to the US 36th TAC Fighter Wing, always a great source of material; Madame Lejeune, wife of the Burgomaster of Büllingen, whose family suffered so much in the battle, but who mobilised her very considerable energy to find me documents and witnesses of those terrible events of over a quarter of a century ago; and finally—naturally—*Obersturmbannfuehrer* Jochen Peiper himself.